Flavors of Summer

Flavors of Summer

Simply delicious food to enjoy on warm days

RYLAND PETERS & SMALL
LONDON • NEW YORK

Senior Designer Toni Kay
Editor Kate Eddison
Production Mai-Ling Collyer
Art Director Leslie Harrington
Editorial Director Julia Charles
Publisher Cindy Richards
Indexer Hilary Bird

First published in 2015 by
Ryland Peters & Small
20–21 Jockey's Fields,
London WC1R 4BW
and
341 E 116th St
New York NY 10029
www.rylandpeters.com

Text © Ryland Peters & Small 2015
and contributors listed on p176
Design and photographs ©
Ryland Peters & Small 2015

UK ISBN: 978-1-84975-606-8
US ISBN: 978-1-84975-634-1

Printed and bound in China

10 9 8 7 6 5 4 3 2 1

A CIP record for this book is available from
the British Library.

US Library of Congress Cataloging-in-
Publication Data has been applied for.

NOTES

• Both British (Metric) and American
(Imperial plus US cups) measurements and
ingredients are included in these recipes for
your convenience, however it is important to
work with one set of measurements and not
alternate between the two within a recipe.
Spellings are primarily British.
• All spoon measurements are level unless
otherwise specified.
• All eggs are medium (UK) or large (US),
unless specified as large, in which case US
extra-large should be used. Uncooked or
partially cooked eggs should not be served
to the very old, frail, young children, pregnant
women or those with compromised immune
systems.
• When a recipe calls for the grated zest of
citrus fruit, buy unwaxed fruit and wash well
before using. If you can only find treated fruit,
scrub well in warm, soapy water and rinse
before using.
• Ovens should be preheated to the specified
temperatures. We recommend using an oven
thermometer. If using a fan-assisted oven,
adjust temperatures according to the
manufacturer's instructions.
• To sterilize jars, wash them in hot, soapy
water and rinse in boiling water. Place in a
large saucepan and cover with hot water.
With the saucepan lid on, bring the water to
a boil and continue boiling for 15 minutes.
Turn off the heat and leave the jars in the hot
water until just before they are to be filled.
Invert the jars onto a clean dish towel to dry.
Sterilize the lids for 5 minutes, by boiling or
according to the manufacturer's instructions.
Jars should be filled and sealed while they
are still hot.

Contents

Sunshine dining

Bright, summer days and long, warm evenings call for food that can be enjoyed at leisure with family and friends. From casual grazing plates to impressive alfresco dinner parties, this book brings together ideas from around the world to celebrate the joy of summer entertaining.

Snacks and Plates to Share brings together nibbles from sun-drenched countries, taking in classic antipasti, tapas, mezze and other delicious mouthfuls. Try Beef and Black Bean Sliders with Corn and Pepper Salsa, Patatas Bravas, Vietnamese Summer Rolls or Sticky Spare Ribs.

Summer Salads is packed with fresh and vibrant recipes that can be served as light meals or appetizers. Nutritious and delicious ideas include Salade Niçoise with Vine-roasted Tomatoes, Sweet Chilli Noodle Salad with Crunchy Asian Greens and Lobster and Tarragon Potato Salad.

For those midday munchies, try something from the Sunshine Lunches chapter, which includes chilled soups, seasonal sandwiches and an array of easily transportable food for picnics. Why not try a refreshing Gazpacho, a Mozzarella Puttanesca Sandwich or pack up portions of Frittata Lorraine for a summer's day out.

One of the best aspects of those long, hot days is the chance for a barbecue or cook-out. Best-ever Barbecue provides plenty of gourmet ideas, from a Classic Beef Burger with Tomato Ketchup and Lettuce to Hot-smoked Creole Salmon.

For more elegant options, look no further than Outdoor Dining, with recipes for alfresco feasts, such as Moroccan-spiced Shoulder of Lamb or Thai Green Curry with Toasted Coconut Rice.

Finish with Desserts and Sweet Treats, from Potted Amaretti Tiramisù to Rosewater Pavlova, and wash it all down with a cooling beverage from Drinks. Try a Peach Iced Tea, or whip up a Mojito for grown-up guests.

Snacks and plates to share

Fried green tomatoes with summer pickles

Green tomatoes lightly tossed in a spicy cornmeal, then fried until crisp and golden brown. Served alongside a beautiful pile of summer pickles, there is nothing better. It's a meal in itself. Don't try to substitute ripe tomatoes — they just aren't the same.

6 large green tomatoes

1 recipe of Fried Green Tomato Spice Mix (see opposite)

vegetable oil, to cook

coarse sea salt, to sprinkle

SUMMER PICKLES

450 g/1 lb. mixed summer vegetables, such as courgette/zucchini, beans, beetroot/beets and (bell) peppers

1 recipe of 'Put-ups' Summer Pickle Brine (see opposite)

SERVES 4-6

To make the pickles, cut the vegetables into bite-size batons and layer in a ceramic baking dish. Pour over the hot 'Put-ups' Summer Pickle Brine, cover, and set aside for 4–24 hours. When ready to eat, remove the vegetables from the brine and pile up in a serving bowl.

Wash the tomatoes under cold water and slice them into 1-cm/½-inch discs. Pour the Fried Green Tomato Spice Mix into a shallow bowl and lightly toss the tomato slices in it.

Heat a cast iron pan over a medium–high heat and coat with vegetable oil. Put a single layer of tomatoes in the pan and cook for about 3–5 minutes until golden brown. Turn the tomatoes over and continue to cook until crispy and golden brown. Remove the cooked tomatoes to a platter and continue to cook the remainder in batches.

Sprinkle liberally with coarse sea salt and serve immediately with a bowl of the Summer Pickles.

Fried green tomato spice mix

This spice mix can be used for lots of dishes. Try coating fish or tossing okra/ladies fingers in it before frying. The cornmeal adds a nice crunch that contrasts with the soft, cooked tomatoes while the Louisiana-style spices pack a flavourful punch.

150 g/1 cup fine polenta/cornmeal

2 tablespoons coarse polenta/cornmeal

½ teaspoon cayenne pepper

½ teaspoon dried garlic powder

½ teaspoon dried chilli flakes/hot pepper flakes

1 teaspoon dried oregano

1 teaspoon dried basil

½ teaspoon ground black pepper

¼ teaspoon table salt

MAKES 300 ML/1¼ CUPS

Put all the ingredients together in a bowl and mix together.

Store the spice mix in a glass jar with a tight-fitting lid for up to 1 month.

Use according to the recipe on page 10, or as preferred.

'Put-ups' summer pickle brine

'Put-ups' is a happy turn of phrase. It is the term used to describe putting up the harvest, when the summer's bounty is preserved for eating through the barren winter months. Summer will jump straight out at you from the jar!

480 ml/2 cups red wine vinegar

100 g/½ cup caster/granulated sugar

1 teaspoon black peppercorns

1 teaspoon yellow mustard seeds

1½ tablespoons sea salt

sterilized glass jars with airtight lids (see page 4)

MAKES 600 ML/2½ CUPS

Put all the ingredients in a non-reactive saucepan and bring to a boil. Use as directed in the recipe on page 10, or as a preserving brine.

To preserve, pour the hot liquid over the tightly packed vegetables in sterilized glass jars and seal. Store in a cool place for up to 1 year.

CHICKEN WINGS

140 g/1 cup plain/all-purpose flour

½ teaspoon paprika

½ teaspoon cayenne pepper

½ teaspoon sea salt

20 chicken wings

RANCH DRESSING

250 ml/1 cup buttermilk, shaken

60 g/¼ cup mayonnaise

3 tablespoons sour cream

3 tablespoons flat leaf parsley, finely chopped

2 tablespoons chives, finely chopped

4 teaspoons white wine vinegar or lemon juice

1 garlic clove, finely chopped

¼ teaspoon garlic powder

½ teaspoon sea salt, plus extra if needed

2 pinches ground black pepper

HOT SAUCE

100 g/½ cup butter

125 ml/½ cup Louisiana hot sauce,
    or other hot pepper sauce

2 pinches ground black pepper

3 pinches garlic powder

vegetable oil, for frying

celery and carrots, for dipping

MAKES 20

Combine the flour, paprika, cayenne pepper and salt in a large resealable food bag. Shake the bag to combine the spices. Next, put the chicken wings in the bag, seal tightly and shake them to coat evenly with the spice mix. Place the bag in the refrigerator for 60–90 minutes.

Place all of the ranch dressing ingredients in a 500-ml/2-cup jar with a tight-fitting lid. Seal tightly and shake to evenly distribute all the ingredients.

Buffalo chicken wings
with homemade ranch dressing

Taking their name from the city in which they originated, Buffalo, New York, Buffalo wings have become an American food staple, often served during sporting events or at late-night bars.

Taste and season with additional salt and pepper as desired. Refrigerate until chilled and the flavours have melded, about 1 hour. The dressing will last up to 3 days in the refrigerator.

Combine the butter, Louisiana or other hot pepper sauce, ground black pepper and garlic powder in a small saucepan over a low heat. Warm until the butter is melted and the ingredients are well blended. Set aside.

In a large, deep, frying pan/skillet, add the vegetable oil to a depth of 2.5–5 cm/1–2 inches and heat to 190°C (375°F) or until the oil is bubbling steadily. Alternatively, use a deep fryer and follow the manufacturer's instructions.

Put the wings into the heated oil and fry them for 10–15 minutes, or until some parts of the wings begin to turn a golden to dark brown colour, and the wings are cooked through.

Remove the wings from the oil and drain on paper towels for a few seconds. Place the wings in a large bowl. Add the hot sauce mixture and stir, tossing the wings to coat them thoroughly.

Serve with the homemade ranch dressing and with a few sticks of celery and carrot.

Southern shrimp hushpuppies
with corn and Poblano relish

Named after the tidbits hunters carry to hush their dogs, these bites will leave you speechless, too.

150 g/1 cup cornmeal

2 tablespoons plain/all-purpose flour

¼ teaspoon bicarbonate of soda/baking soda

3 teaspoons baking powder

½ teaspoon sea salt

½ teaspoon ground white pepper

180 ml/¾ cup buttermilk

1 egg, lightly beaten

225 g/8 oz. prawns/shrimp, deveined

140 g/1 cup fresh corn kernels

2 spring onions/scallions, thinly sliced

1 jalapeño pepper, finely chopped

vegetable oil, for deep frying

TO SERVE

sea salt

Corn and Poblano Relish (see right)

an oil-resistant thermometer

MAKES 20

Place the cornmeal, flour, bicarbonate of soda/baking soda, baking powder, salt and pepper in a large bowl and mix together. Pour in the buttermilk and egg and mix together. Add the prawns/shrimp, corn, onions and jalapeño and mix well to combine all the ingredients.

Place a deep frying pan/skillet over medium–high heat and add enough oil to come three-quarters of the way up the pan. Heat the oil to 185°C (365°F). Using a small ice cream scoop and working in batches, drop the hushpuppies into the hot fat. Sauté for 5 minutes, or until golden and cooked through. Transfer each batch to a warm serving plate.

Sprinkle with coarse sea salt and serve with Corn and Poblano Relish.

Corn and Poblano relish

This relish is sweet and tangy and has a lot of spice. It is delicious spooned over tacos, burgers, hot dogs and any kind of grilled foods.

3 Poblano chillies/chiles

2 tablespoons olive oil, plus extra for oiling

2 garlic cloves, finely chopped

1 red onion, finely diced

1 red (bell) pepper, finely diced

420 g/3 cups corn kernels

6 spring onions/scallions, thinly sliced

grated zest and freshly squeezed juice of 1 lime

1 tablespoon dried chilli flakes/hot pepper flakes

150 g/¾ cup soft light brown sugar

425 ml/1¾ cups apple cider vinegar

sea salt and cracked black pepper

sterilized glass jars with airtight lids (see page 4)

MAKES 950 ML/4 CUPS

Place a lightly oiled large cast-iron pan over high heat until smoking. Add the Poblano chillies, lower the heat, and cook until the skins are charred and blistered. Remove from the pan and let cool.

Chop the Poblano chillies and set aside. Return the pan to a medium heat, add the olive oil, garlic, onion and (bell) pepper and sauté for 5 minutes. Add the Poblanos, corn, spring onions/scallions, lime zest and juice and dried chilli flakes/hot pepper flakes, and stir. Add the sugar, pour in the vinegar and season with salt and pepper. Stir and bring to the boil, then reduce the heat and simmer for 15–20 minutes.

Pack the relish into the jars, leaving a 5-mm/½-inch space at the top. Tap the jars on the counter to get rid of air pockets. Wipe the jars clean and screw on the lids. Fill a canning kettle with enough water to cover the height of the jars by 5 cm/ 2 inches and bring to the boil. Place the jars in the water bath. Cover with a lid and once the water has come back to the boil, seal for 10 minutes. Remove the jars from the water bath and transfer to a cooling rack. Check to make sure that the centres of the lids are concaved. Store unopened in a cool, dark place for up to 12 months.

Sticky spare ribs

Finger-licking good! You'll need a pile of napkins for these. Serve with Vietnamese Summer Rolls (page 16), Thai-style Mini Fish Cakes (page 17) and ice-cold beers for a summer party.

1 kg/2 lbs. short or loin pork ribs/country-style pork spare ribs

4 garlic cloves, crushed

2 tablespoons grated fresh ginger

4 tablespoons clear honey

2 tablespoons soy sauce

2 tablespoons hoisin sauce

2 tablespoons sweet chilli/chili sauce

2 tablespoons tamarind paste

¼ teaspoon Chinese five-spice powder

SERVES 4-6

Place the ribs in a saucepan of water, bring up to the boil and simmer for 5–10 minutes, then drain.

Mix the remaining ingredients together in a large bowl, add the ribs and stir thoroughly to coat. Let cool and allow to marinate for about 30 minutes.

Preheat the oven to 190°C (375°F) Gas 5.

Tip the ribs and marinade into a large roasting pan, cover with foil and cook on the middle shelf of the preheated oven for about 20 minutes. Remove the foil, turn the ribs over, basting them with the marinade, and cook for 20 minutes more until sticky and browned all over. Allow to rest for a couple of minutes before serving with plenty of napkins.

Vietnamese summer rolls

These flow-fat rolls are a far cry from the familiar deep-fried Chinese version. Fresh, cool and completely delicious, they are perfect for a summer's day and can be made the morning of your picnic, stored and carried in an airtight container to be served on the move.

25 g/1 oz. fine rice vermicelli

6 rice-paper discs or wrappers (available in Oriental stores)

200 g/7 oz. cooked prawns/shrimp, halved lengthways if large

a bunch of fresh mint, stalks removed

a bunch of fresh coriander/cilantro or Thai basil, stalks removed

2 carrots, grated

30 g/½ cup beansprouts

hoisin dipping sauce, to serve

MAKES 6

Break up the rice vermicelli into smaller lengths, about 8–10 cm/3–4 inches, and cook according to the package instructions. Refresh the noodles under cold water, then leave to drain.

Now get ready to roll. It's best to do this with an assembly line: start with a large shallow dish of warm water to soak the rice-paper discs in; next, you will need a plate covered with a clean dish towel, on which to drape them once soaked; then the prawns/shrimp, herb leaves, vermicelli and other fresh ingredients, each in a separate bowl.

Soak a rice-paper disc in the warm water for 15 seconds until translucent and pliable, then move to the plate. Start to make a pile of the ingredients in the middle of the disc. I usually start with 2 whole mint leaves, placed shiny side down, then the noodles, grated carrot and beansprouts, then 2–3 prawns/shrimp, and finally a good handful of coriander/cilantro (the trick to a good summer roll is not being shy with your herbs).

Roll up tightly from the bottom, fold in the sides, then finish rolling up the cylinder. Repeat the process for each roll, topping up the warm water when necessary. It is best to make each roll individually as the rice-paper discs tend to be quite sticky. Pack the rolls into a plastic container and keep cool until ready to serve, accompanied by the hoisin dipping sauce.

125 g/4 oz. skinless, boneless cod
    or other white fish
150 g/5 oz. raw peeled and deveined
    prawns/shrimp
100 g/1 cup grated fresh coconut
1 fresh red chilli/chile
4 spring onions/scallions, sliced
1 tablespoon freshly chopped coriander/cilantro
1 tablespoon Thai red curry paste
pinch of salt
2–3 tablespoons sunflower oil, for frying
lime wedges, to serve

DIPPING SAUCE

125 ml/½ cup rice wine vinegar
100 g/½ cup caster/granulated sugar
1 fresh red chilli/chile, finely chopped
1 carrot
3-cm/1-inch piece of cucumber
1 tablespoon roasted peanuts

SERVES 2–4

Thai-style mini fish cakes
with cucumber and peanut dipping sauce

These little fish cakes can be prepared and cooked in advance, covered with foil, then reheated in a moderate oven. Serve alongside Vietnamese Summer Rolls (page 16) and Sticky Spare Ribs (page 15), and even a bowl of sticky jasmine or egg-fried rice.

Prepare the dipping sauce first. Pour the vinegar into a small saucepan, add the sugar and bring slowly to the boil to dissolve the sugar. Simmer until the syrup thickens slightly. Add the chilli/chile, remove from the heat and let cool. Peel and finely dice the carrot. Scrape the seeds from the cucumber, discard, then finely dice the flesh. Roughly chop the peanuts. Add everything to the cooled chilli/chile syrup.

To make the fish cakes, cut the fish into large chunks and place in a food processor with the prawns/shrimp and

coconut. Whizz until combined and nearly smooth. Remove the seeds from the chilli/chile and finely chop the flesh. Tip into a bowl with the fish mixture, spring onions/scallions, coriander/cilantro, curry paste and salt. Mix well. Divide the mixture into 8–10 evenly sized portions and, using wet hands, shape into patties.

Heat the oil in a frying pan/skillet over medium heat and fry the fish cakes in 2 or 3 batches until golden brown, about 2 minutes on each side. Drain on paper towels and serve with lime wedges and the dipping sauce.

Tomato keftedes with tzatziki

400 g/14 oz. ripe cherry tomatoes
½ red onion, very finely chopped
5 g/¼ cup basil, chopped
10 g/½ cup mint, chopped
1 teaspoon dried oregano
5 g/¼ cup flat leaf parsley, chopped
100 g/¾ cup self-raising/rising flour
250 ml/1 cup olive oil
750 ml/3 cups sunflower or canola oil
salt and black pepper

TZATZIKI

1 cucumber
350 g/12 oz. Greek/US strained plain yogurt
2 tablespoons lemon juice
2 garlic cloves, finely chopped or grated
1 tablespoon extra virgin olive oil

MAKES 16

A combination of onions and green herbs bound together with tomato flesh and flour, then fried, these vegetarian tomato fritters make a lovely addition to a mezze platter.

For the Tzatziki, cut the cucumber in half lengthways and use a teaspoon to scrape out the seeds. Grate the 2 halves into a clean dish towel. Gather up the edges and squeeze out as much excess liquid as you can. Whisk together the yogurt, lemon juice, garlic and olive oil. Add the squeezed cucumber flesh and stir.

To make the tomato keftedes, put the tomatoes in a large bowl and pinch them so that the juices spurt out (be careful to pinch them facing downwards, otherwise you'll end up with pulp in your eye). Keep pinching and tearing at the flesh until you're left with a pile of seeds, juices and pulp.

Add the onion, basil, mint, oregano, parsley and salt and pepper to the pulp.

You can use a potato masher at this point to make sure everything is thoroughly incorporated.

Add half the flour and stir. Add the second half slowly. You want a thick and sticky paste the texture of a thick batter.

Heat the oils in a deep, heavy-based pan until small bubbles form on the surface. Make sure the oil is at least 5 cm/ 2 inches deep. Use a greased tablespoon to drop in spoonfuls of the batter. After 30 seconds, rotate the fritters so they don't stick to the bottom. Fry for 30 seconds more, or until the outside is crispy and deep red. Drain well on paper towels. Fry no more than 3 at a time.

Season the fritters with salt and serve hot with Tzatziki.

Sweet potato falafel with homemade toum

These Lebanese falafel are updated with earthy sweet potatoes and toum sauce is an absolute must. You can buy falafel from any good deli or supermarket, but it's fun to make your own and they always taste miles better when home-cooked.

3 medium sweet potatoes

1 x 410-g/14-oz. can chickpeas, drained and rinsed

180 g/1¼ cups gram (chickpea) flour

1 banana shallot, or 2 regular shallots, finely diced

3 garlic cloves, crushed

1½ teaspoons ground cumin

2 teaspoons ground coriander

3 handfuls of fresh coriander/cilantro, finely chopped

freshly squeezed juice of 1 lemon

sea salt and ground black pepper

a sprinkling of sesame seeds (optional)

TOUM GARLIC SAUCE

245 g/1 cup Greek/US strained plain yogurt

2 tablespoons mayonnaise

½ tablespoon extra virgin olive oil

2 sprigs of fresh mint, stalks removed and leaves very finely chopped

2 garlic cloves, crushed

a squeeze of fresh lemon juice

a pinch of sea salt

TO SERVE

6 whole pita breads

2 tablespoons houmous, or to taste

½ green cabbage, raw, shredded

3 tomatoes, sliced

3 baby Gem/Bibb lettuces, leaves

a baking sheet, greased and lined with baking parchment

SERVES 6

Preheat the oven to 200°C (400°F) Gas 6.

Roast the sweet potatoes in their skins for about 1 hour until cooked through. (Alternatively, you can microwave the sweet potatoes, whole, for 15–20 minutes until tender.) Leave the potatoes until cool enough to handle, peel off and discard the skin, then chop roughly.

Put the cooked potatoes, chickpeas, gram flour, shallot, garlic, cumin, ground coriander, fresh coriander/cilantro and lemon juice into a large mixing bowl. Season well with salt and pepper, then mash with a fork or potato masher until smooth. (You can also do this in a food processor if you have one.) The mixture should be sticky to touch but not wet. If the mixture is still quite sloppy you could add a little more gram flour.

Using a dessertspoon, scoop spoonfuls of the mix and shape into 18 balls, about the size of a ping-pong ball. Arrange the balls a little way apart on the prepared baking sheet, then flatten each into a patty. Pop the baking sheet in the fridge for 1 hour, or in the freezer for 20 minutes if you are pushed for time.

To make the toum garlic sauce, in a mixing bowl, whisk the yogurt and mayonnaise together until smooth and creamy. While whisking, slowly pour in the olive oil. Finally, add the chopped mint, crushed garlic, lemon juice and a pinch of sea salt, and give it a final mix until everything is well combined.

When the patties are chilled, sprinkle over the sesame seeds, if using, then pop them in the oven and bake at 200°C

(400°F) Gas 6 for 15 minutes until lovely and brown all over.

To serve, toast the pitas, then split them open. Spread a thin layer of houmous on the inside before stuffing with cabbage, tomatoes, lettuce and 3 of the falafels. Top with plenty of Toum Garlic Sauce just before serving.

Mezze platter
of baba ghanoush with flatbreads

Baba ghanoush is a gorgeous alternative to houmous. The trick to making a show-stopping baba ghanoush is to roast the aubergines/eggplants until the skin is blackened, which will give the dish a rich, heady smokiness. You can serve it with vegetable crudités as well as flatbreads, if you wish.

4 aubergines/eggplants

2 garlic cloves, crushed

freshly squeezed juice of 1 lemon

1 generous tablespoon tahini paste

2–3 tablespoons olive oil

sea salt and ground black pepper

a sprinkling of pomegranate seeds, chopped fresh coriander/cilantro, ½ teaspoon toasted cumin seeds, or a teaspoon of harissa paste, to garnish

FLATBREADS

½ teaspoon dried/active dry yeast

250 ml/1 cup warm water

500 g/4 cups plain/all-purpose or wholemeal/whole-wheat flour, plus extra for dusting

400 g/1⅔ cups plain yogurt

40 ml/3 tablespoons olive oil (plus extra for brushing the flatbreads, if cooking on a griddle)

sea salt

a baking sheet, lightly greased, or a griddle pan

a baking sheet, greased with olive oil

SERVES 6

Preheat the oven to 200°C (400°F) Gas 6.

Put the whole aubergines/eggplants on the prepared baking sheet, side by side, and roast in the preheated oven for about 30 minutes, or until the skins are blistered and blackened. Remove the aubergines/eggplants from the oven and let cool.

Once cool, scrape all the flesh from the aubergines/eggplants into a mixing bowl, discarding the charred skins. Add the crushed garlic, most of the lemon juice (a little flesh of the lemon is also quite nice), the tahini and 2 tablespoons of the olive oil. Using a fork, mash up the flesh as much as you can until everything is well incorporated into a chunky purée. Season with a pinch of salt and pepper and taste. It should be smoky, sweet, garlicky, tangy. If the paste is too thick or the taste of garlic is too pungent, add a little more lemon juice and olive oil. Set the baba ghanoush aside while you make the flatbreads.

When you are ready to serve, sprinkle your chosen garnish on top to add colour and flavour, drizzle with a little olive oil and serve with the flatbreads.

To make the flatbreads, in a jug/cup dissolve the yeast in the warm water, and set aside for 10 minutes.

Sift the flour into a large mixing bowl and make a well in the middle. Add the yogurt and mix well. Now gently pour a little of the water and yeast mixture into the well in the flour, along with a good glug of the olive oil. Knead the dough with your hands to combine, bringing the flour into the middle of the bowl and adding a little more of the yeast mixture and the olive oil at a time. When all the ingredients are combined, bring the dough out of the bowl and knead it on a floured surface for about 10 minutes, until it is shiny and smooth. Place the dough back in the bowl, cover with a clean dish towel and leave in a warm, dry place for 1½–2 hours, until almost doubled in size.

When the dough has proved, give it a final knead to dispel any air, then divide the mixture into 6 balls. On a floured surface, roll out each ball to approximately 5 mm/¼ inch thick and sprinkle with sea salt.

Here, you can either preheat your oven to 200°C (400°F) Gas 6, put the flatbreads on the prepared baking sheet and bake for 6–8 minutes; or brush the breads with olive oil on both sides and place on a smoking hot griddle pan for around 1–2 minutes on each side, until golden. Serve on a platter with the Baba Ghanoush.

GARLIC-INFUSED OLIVE OIL

8 garlic cloves, unpeeled

65 ml/2 oz. light olive oil

65 ml/2 oz. extra virgin olive oil

2 tablespoons balsamic vinegar

WARM MARINATED OLIVES

100 g/3½ oz. large green olives, such as Sicilian

100 g/3½ oz. small black olives, such as Ligurian

250 ml/1 cup extra virgin olive oil

2 sprigs of fresh thyme

2 dried red chillies

1 bay leaf

2 thin slices of orange peel

good crusty bread, to serve

SERVES 6–8

Garlic-infused olive oil and warm marinated olives

This sharing plate is simplicity itself to put together and absolutely no preparation is needed once your guests arrive. Lay out the platter and let it sit at room temperature for a short while before serving, and have the all-important drinks at the ready, too. A fruity sangria would be the perfect accompaniment.

To make the garlic-infused olive oil, put the garlic cloves and light olive oil in a small saucepan and cook over a medium heat for 5 minutes. Remove from the heat and let cool. Add the extra virgin olive oil and vinegar and transfer to a serving bowl.

Put the olives in a small, heatproof bowl. Put the oil, thyme, chillies, bay leaf and orange peel in a small saucepan. Set over a medium heat. As soon as you hear the herbs starting to sizzle in the oil, remove the saucepan from the heat and pour the mixture over the olives. Let cool for 20 minutes.

To serve, arrange the still-warm garlic-infused oil, olives and bread on a platter. Let your guests help themselves.

Gravadlax with gin and beetroot

Any luxurious summer party should start with a canapé or two, and this scrumptious Scandinavian delicacy is a must for any celebratory feast. The salmon is easy to prepare and can be made well in advance.

700 g/1½ lb. piece of salmon, filleted but skin left on

75 ml/5 tablespoons gin

½ tablespoon fennel seeds

½ tablespoon caraway seeds

½ tablespoon ground pink pepper

1 tablespoon crushed juniper berries

50 g/¼ caster/granulated sugar

170 g/¾ cup sea salt flakes

2 beetroot/beets, peeled and grated

grated zest of 1 lemon

a bunch of fresh dill, chopped

SERVES 8

Line a large tray with clingfilm/plastic wrap before laying the salmon skin-side down on the tray. Run your hand gently over the flesh and remove any remaining bones with tweezers. Pour over the gin and rub it into the flesh really well.

Using a pestle and mortar or a food processor, crush the seeds, pepper and juniper berries until they are fine. Add the sugar and flaked sea salt, and mix well before sprinkling this evenly over the salmon fillet. Next, sprinkle over the grated beetroot/beets and the salt and spice mixture, and then grate the zest of 1 lemon evenly over it too. Lastly, layer on the freshly chopped dill. The whole salmon side should be covered. Lay another piece of clingfilm/plastic wrap over the top and wrap the fish tightly, keeping the fillet in the tray for any leaking juices to escape into. Lay a chopping/cutting board or heavy tray on top of the salmon to flatten and weight the fillet down, then leave the fish to marinate in the refrigerator for 48 hours.

After this time, remove the clingfilm/plastic wrap and pour away the brine that is in the tray. Push the salt, spices, beetroot/beets and dill off the fish and discard them. Wash away any excess topping with water, if you need to, and pat the gravadlax down with paper towels. Well wrapped, the gravadlax will keep in your refrigerator for up to 2 weeks.

To serve, place the fish skin-side down on a large chopping/cutting board. Using a sharp, narrow-bladed knife, start at the tail end and separate the skin from the fillet. Discard the skin and remove any brown bits of flesh from underneath. Now, with the knife on a diagonal slant, slice the gravadlax into very thin sheets.

Buckwheat blinis with gravadlax and horseradish cream

These buckwheat blinis, topped with horseradish cream and cured salmon gravadlax, taste delicious and look great, too.

400 ml/1⅔ cups whole milk
sea salt
300 g/2¼ cups buckwheat flour
100 g/¾ cup plain/all-purpose flour
30 g/1 oz. fresh yeast
2 eggs, separated
200 ml/¾ cup ale
butter, for frying
Gravadlax (see opposite), to serve

HORSERADISH CREAM

2 tablespoons finely grated fresh horseradish
350 g/1½ cups crème fraîche
a good pinch of English mustard powder

SERVES 8

In a saucepan set over a low heat, warm the milk very gently until it is tepid.

In a large mixing bowl, put ½ teaspoon of salt in the bottom, followed by the flours and lastly crumble the yeast on top. Make a well in the middle and pour in the tepid milk and the two egg yolks, whisking rapidly until smooth. Add half of the ale and mix well to a smooth thick batter. Cover the bowl with clingfilm/plastic wrap and leave in a warm place for at least 2 hours until doubled in volume.

In a separate bowl, whisk the egg whites until stiff but not dry.

Add the remaining ale to the batter, mix slowly, then gently fold in the egg whites. Cover and let stand for 30 minutes.

Heat a good dollop of butter in a non-stick frying pan/skillet set over medium–high heat, and swirl the pan so the melted butter covers the base. Use a dessertspoon to spoon dollops of batter into the pan, spaced well apart, and fry until little bubbles appear on top. When the edges of the blinis are golden, use a palette knife to flip the pancakes over and cook the other sides for a 1–2 minutes. When cooked, transfer the blinis to a paper towel to soak up any excess grease and leave to cool. Repeat, cooking batches of blinis until all the batter is used up. Pack in an airtight container. They are best eaten on the day of making.

For the horseradish cream, mix all the ingredients together and season. Arrange on the buckwheat blinis with a dollop of horseradish cream and a tiny sprig of chives or dill for prettiness.

Crispy calamari with butter beans and chorizo

2 tablespoons olive oil

1 onion, thinly sliced

1 garlic clove, crushed

½ teaspoon cumin seeds, lightly crushed

a pinch of dried chilli flakes/hot pepper flakes

½ teaspoon dried oregano

100 g/3½ oz. cooking chorizo, diced

200-g/6½-oz. can chopped tomatoes

400-g/14-oz. can butter/lima beans, drained

2 tablespoons freshly chopped flat leaf parsley

250 g/8 oz. small squid tubes

2 tablespoons plain/all-purpose flour

sugar, for seasoning (optional)

sea salt and freshly ground black pepper

SERVES 4

Try to use small, tender baby squid rings with tentacles for this recipe and serve as part of a meal with the Assorted Focaccia Crostini (page 26) or Albóndigas (page 32).

Heat half the oil in a medium saucepan, add the onion and cook for 4–5 minutes until tender but not coloured. Add the garlic, cumin, chillies and oregano, and continue to cook for a further minute. Add the diced chorizo and cook until lightly browned and the onions have started to caramelize.

Add the chopped tomatoes and drained beans, and simmer for about 20 minutes, or until thick. Add the parsley and season with salt and black pepper, plus a pinch of sugar if the sauce needs it to balance the tomatoes.

Cut the squid into 1-cm/½-inch thick rings, pat dry on paper towels and toss in seasoned flour. Heat the remaining oil in a large frying pan/skillet, and, when it's smoking hot, add half the prepared squid. Cook for 2–3 minutes, until golden brown and cooked through. Remove from the pan and cook the remaining squid. Spoon the calamari on top of the chorizo and butter-bean mixture, and serve immediately.

Assorted focaccia crostini

Focaccia is one of the tastiest breads to make, and so easy that it's a crime not to bake it yourself. This focaccia can be made in advance and sliced just before serving.

Mix together the flour, yeast and fine salt in a large bowl. Add 1 tablespoon of the olive oil and the water and mix to a soft dough. Lightly dust the work surface with flour, turn the dough out of the bowl and knead for 10 minutes, or until smooth and elastic. Shape the dough into a neat, smooth ball, return to the bowl and cover with clingfilm/plastic wrap. Leave in a warm place for 1 hour, or until doubled in size. Lightly oil the baking pan. Dust the work surface with flour, turn the dough out and knead for 30 seconds. Roll the dough into a rectangle to fit in the baking pan. Lay the dough inside the pan. Cover with

oiled clingfilm/plastic wrap and leave in a warm place for about 1 hour, or until doubled in size. Preheat the oven to 220°C (425°F) Gas 7. Dimple the surface of the dough with your fingertips, drizzle the remaining olive oil all over it and sprinkle the rosemary and salt flakes over the top. Bake in the preheated oven for about 20 minutes, or until golden brown and well risen. Let cool in the pan for about 10 minutes, then transfer to a wire rack. Cut the focaccia into finger-width slices, toast both sides on a ridged stovetop griddle/grill pan and top with one of the following toppings:

For the Garlic Mushrooms, heat the oil and butter in a frying pan/skillet, add the shallot and cook over medium heat until translucent. Add the mushrooms, season, cook until tender and stir through the parsley. Rub the garlic clove over the toasted bread and pile the mixture on top. Drizzle with olive oil. Serve warm.

For the Mediterranean Tomatoes, chop the tomatoes and red (bell) pepper. Add the basil and olives and gently stir through the mozzarella. Rub the garlic clove over the toasted bread and pile the mixture on top. Drizzle with olive oil. Serve hot.

For the Beans and Mint, whizz the cooked beans or peas in a food processor to a coarse purée. Stir in the mint, lemon and feta and season. Rub the garlic clove over the toasted bread and pile the mixture on top. Drizzle with olive oil. Serve hot.

500 g/4 cups strong white bread flour

7-g sachet/package or 3 level teaspoons fast-action/instant dried yeast

1 teaspoon fine sea salt

4 tablespoons extra virgin olive oil

300 ml/1¼ cups hand-hot water

2 tablespoons fresh rosemary leaves

2 generous teaspoons sea salt flakes

GARLIC MUSHROOMS

1 tablespoon olive oil

1 tablespoon unsalted butter

1 shallot, finely chopped

250 g/8 oz. mixed wild mushrooms

1 tablespoon freshly chopped flat leaf parsley

1 garlic clove

MEDITERRANEAN TOMATOES

4 ripe tomatoes

1 roasted red (bell) pepper, from a jar

1 tablespoon fresh basil leaves, torn

1 tablespoon mixed pitted olives, chopped

100 g/3½ oz. buffalo mozzarella, torn

1 garlic clove

BEANS AND MINT

175 g/1⅓ cups cooked broad/fava beans and/or peas, crushed

1 tablespoon freshly chopped mint

grated zest of ½ unwaxed lemon

100 g/3½ oz. feta, crumbled

1 garlic clove

a 20 x 30-cm/8 x 12-inch baking pan

SERVES 4-6

Asparagus wrapped in Parma ham with a lemon mayonnaise

Asparagus season is always keenly anticipated, and rightly so — summer would not be complete without it! Enjoy it at its best, paired with the contrasting textures of salty Parma ham and a creamy lemon mayonnaise. It is a quick recipe to prepare yet elegant enough for summer entertaining.

Set a large saucepan of salted water over a high heat and bring to the boil.

Trim or break off the base of each asparagus spear, then poach them in the water for 90 seconds only. Plunge the spears into ice cold water to refresh, then lay them on paper towels to dry off.

Wrap a piece of Parma ham/prosciutto around the middle of each asparagus spear, keeping the flowered head exposed. Keep them cool until ready to eat.

To make the lemon mayonnaise, simply whizz up the egg yolk, lemon juice and a pinch of salt and white pepper in a food processor. While the machine is still running, very slowly dribble in the olive oil until it is all incorporated. When you have a lovely smooth texture, mix in the lemon zest.

Serve the asparagus with a grinding of black pepper, and serve the lemon mayonnaise on the side for dipping.

Note If the mayonnaise starts to separate or go lumpy at all, add ½ teaspoon of white wine vinegar before resuming adding the oil.

16 spears of fresh, trimmed asparagus

8 slices Parma ham/prosciutto, sliced in half widthways

LEMON MAYONNAISE

3 very fresh egg yolks

freshly squeezed juice and finely grated zest of 1 unwaxed lemon

150 ml/⅔ cup extra virgin olive oil

sea salt and ground white and black pepper

SERVES 4

Arancini with pecorino, porcini and mozzarella

You can use leftover risotto for these rice balls if you happen to have any, but they are so delicious it's worth making the risotto specially. They can be prepared and rolled in advance; coat them in breadcrumbs and fry just before serving.

Soak the porcini in a small bowl of boiling water for about 15 minutes, or until soft. Drain well on paper towels and chop finely.

Heat the olive oil and butter in a medium saucepan and add the shallots, garlic and chopped porcini. Cook over low–medium heat until soft but not coloured. Add the rice to the pan and stir to coat well in the buttery mixture. Gradually add the vegetable stock – add it one ladleful at a time, and as the stock is absorbed by the rice, add another ladleful, stirring as you do so. Continue cooking in this way until the rice is al dente and the stock is used up. Remove the pan from the heat, add the pecorino and herbs and season well with salt and black pepper. Tip the risotto into a bowl and let cool completely.

Once the rice is cold, divide it into walnut-sized pieces and roll into balls. Taking one ball at a time, flatten it into a disc in the palm of your hand, press some diced mozzarella in the middle and wrap the rice around it to completely encase the cheese. Shape into a neat ball. Repeat with the remaining risotto.

Tip the flour, beaten eggs and breadcrumbs into separate shallow bowls. Roll the rice balls first in the flour, then coat well in the eggs and finally, roll them in the breadcrumbs to completely coat.

Fill a deep-fat fryer with sunflower oil or pour oil to a depth of about 5 cm/ 2 inches into a deep saucepan. Heat until a cube of bread sizzles and browns in about 5 seconds. Cook the arancini, in batches, in the hot oil for 3–4 minutes or until crisp, hot and golden brown. Drain on paper towels.

15 g/½ oz. dried porcini mushrooms

1 tablespoon olive oil

2 tablespoons unsalted butter

2 shallots, finely chopped

1 fat garlic clove, crushed

250 g/1¼ cups risotto rice (arborio or carnaroli)

750–850 ml/3–3½ cups hot vegetable stock

40 g/⅓ cup grated Pecorino

1 tablespoon freshly chopped flat leaf parsley or oregano

125 g/4 oz. mozzarella, diced

100 g/¾ cup plain/all-purpose flour

2 eggs, lightly beaten

200 g/2 cups fresh, fine breadcrumbs

about 1 litre/4 cups sunflower oil, for frying

sea salt and freshly ground black pepper

MAKES 16

Beef carpaccio
with cherry tomato, basil and lemon dressing

Carpaccio of beef is one of those rare dishes that manages to satisfy the inner carnivore while still being seen as a light, diet-friendly choice. One thing's for sure: this recipe is delicious and perfect as a summer appetizer.

250 g/9 oz. beef fillet (ask your butcher for a piece about 8–10 cm/3¼–4 inches thick)

a good handful of cherry tomatoes

a small bunch of fresh basil

100 ml/⅓ cup/6 tablespoons extra virgin olive oil

½ garlic clove, crushed

freshly squeezed juice of 1 lemon

a large handful of rocket/arugula

sea salt and freshly ground black pepper

Parmesan cheese, shaved, to serve

a handful of pine nuts, toasted (optional), to serve

SERVES 4

Freeze the beef fillet for around 45 minutes. This will help make it far easier to slice, and while it's firming up you can prepare the dressing.

Cut the tomatoes into quarters and roughly chop or tear the basil. Mix them together with half the oil and the crushed garlic. Season with salt and pepper.

Mix the remaining olive oil with the lemon juice, adding a little extra salt and pepper to taste. The easiest way by far is to put them into an empty jam jar (or anything with a secure lid or top) and shake it like crazy. Alternatively, you could whisk the mix very quickly using a fork or small whisk. The secret here is to emulsify the two liquids so that they become one sauce rather than just droplets of lemon juice floating in oil.

Take the beef out of the freezer and slice it as thinly as possible. You should almost be able to see through the meat. If you're having difficulty getting it really thin, you can always put each slice between two pieces of clingfilm/plastic wrap and flatten each one with a rolling pin.

To serve, lay the carpaccio slices on a serving platter, trying not to let them overlap too much. Arrange the tomato mixture, rocket/arugula and Parmesan shavings over the beef, along with a few good turns of the pepper mill. Give the lemon-oil emulsion another good stir or shake and drizzle it over the dish. You could also scatter pine nuts across the plate for extra bite.

Beef and black bean sliders with corn and pepper salsa

Capture the taste of South America wherever you are with these delicious beef sliders. Served with spicy corn and pepper salsa and tangy Lime Mayo (below, left), these are guaranteed to create a fiesta of flavours for your tastebuds.

1 tablespoon canned black beans
1 spring onion/scallion, sliced
1 garlic clove, finely chopped
2 teaspoons tomato purée/paste
a pinch of cayenne pepper
1 tablespoon chopped fresh coriander/cilantro
200 g/7 oz. lean minced/ground beef
40 g/3 tablespoons cooked and cooled
    long grain rice
1 tablespoon olive or vegetable oil
a pinch of sea salt and freshly ground
    black pepper

CORN AND PEPPER SALSA

2 large corn cobs
3 tablespoons vegetable oil
4 spring onions/scallions, sliced
freshly squeezed juice of 1 lime
6 Peppadew peppers, diced
2 tablespoons finely chopped coriander/cilantro
a dash of chilli/chili sauce
sea salt and freshly ground black pepper

TO SERVE

4 mini poppyseed rolls
Lime Mayo (see left)

MAKES 4

To make the corn and pepper salsa, cut down the sides of the corn cobs with a sharp knife to remove the kernels. Heat 2 teaspoons of the oil in a frying pan/skillet set over medium heat. Add the corn and cook for 2–3 minutes until it begins to brown. Add the spring onions/scallions and cook for 1 minute. Transfer to a bowl and let cool.

Add the lime juice, peppers, coriander/cilantro and the remaining oil, and mix well. Add a dash of chilli sauce and season with salt and pepper.

To make the sliders, blitz the black beans, spring onion/scallion, garlic, tomato purée/paste, cayenne pepper and coriander/cilantro in a food processor. Pour the mixture into a mixing bowl, add the beef and work together with your hands until evenly mixed. Add the cooled rice, season with salt and pepper and mix again.

Divide the beef mixture into quarters and shape into four slider patties. Press each slider down to make them nice and flat.

Heat the oil in a frying pan/skillet and fry the sliders over medium–high heat for 4 minutes on each side, or until cooked through.

Slice the mini poppyseed rolls in half and spread the bottom half of each with Lime Mayo. Put a cooked slider on top of each and add a large spoonful of Corn and Pepper Salsa. Finish the sliders with the lids of the rolls and serve.

Lime mayo

3 egg yolks
2 teaspoons Dijon mustard
2 teaspoons white wine vinegar
or freshly squeezed lemon juice
½ teaspoon sea salt
300 ml/1¼ cups olive oil
1 teaspoon freshly squeezed lime juice
1 teaspoon finely grated lime zest
a pinch of freshly ground black pepper

MAKES APPROXIMATELY 400 ML/ 1¾ CUPS

Put the egg yolks, mustard, vinegar, lemon juice, zest, salt and pepper in a food processor and blend until foaming. With the blade running, gradually pour in the oil through a funnel until thick and glossy. If it is too thick, add a little water. Adjust the seasoning to taste. Store in the refrigerator for up to 3 days.

Lamb and mint sliders
with roast potatoes and watercress

Create a roast-lamb dinner in miniature form with these gourmet sliders. They taste great in a bun, but even better served inside roast potato rounds.

3 tablespoons olive oil

8 roughly-equal rounds of potato, unpeeled

200 g/7 oz. lean minced/ground lamb

6 fresh mint leaves, finely chopped

3 tablespoons fresh breadcrumbs

1 tablespoon beaten egg

a pinch of sea salt and freshly ground black pepper

TO SERVE

a handful of watercress or rocket/arugula

4 cocktail sticks/toothpicks

MAKES 4

Preheat the oven to 180°C (350°F) Gas 4.

Sprinkle 1 tablespoon of the oil on a baking sheet and lay the potato slices on top, turn to coat and sprinkle with black pepper. Bake in the oven for 25 minutes until brown and crisp. Remove from the oven and set aside until cool enough to handle.

Put the lamb in a bowl with the mint, breadcrumbs, egg and salt and pepper. Work together with your hands until evenly mixed. Divide the mixture into quarters and shape into four slider patties. Press each slider down to make them nice and flat.

Heat the remaining oil in a frying pan/skillet and fry the sliders over medium–high heat for 4 minutes on each side until cooked through.

Put one potato round on each serving plate and put a cooked slider on top of each. Top with a few leaves of watercress and finish with another potato round. Put a cocktail stick/toothpick through the middle of each slider to hold them together and serve.

Albóndigas with spiced tomato sauce

Prepare these flavourful meatballs in their spiced tomato sauce ahead and reheat in a covered casserole dish before serving. They actually taste better if you make them 24 hours in advance.

Heat 2 tablespoons of the oil in a frying pan/skillet and fry the onions until soft. Add the garlic and oregano and continue to cook for 1 minute. Scoop half the onions into a bowl and set aside to cool.

Add the crushed dried chillies and ground cumin to the pan and cook for 30 seconds. Add the red wine, chopped tomatoes and orange peel and cook gently for about 30 minutes, or until the sauce has thickened slightly. Season well with salt, pepper and the sugar, to balance the flavours. Remove from the heat and set aside while you prepare the albóndigas.

To make the albóndigas, remove the skin from the sausages and add the meat to the reserved cooled, cooked onions along with the beef, paprika, ground cumin, parsley, egg, breadcrumbs and milk. Using your hands, mix until combined, season well with salt and pepper, then roll into 20 walnut-sized balls.

Heat the remaining oil in a large frying pan/skillet and brown the albóndigas in batches, adding more oil if necessary.

Add the albóndigas to the spiced tomato sauce and cook gently over low heat for a further 30 minutes. Sprinkle chopped parsley over the top before serving.

200 g/6½ oz. good-quality pork sausages

350 g/12 oz. lean minced/ground beef

1 teaspoon Spanish smoked paprika

½ teaspoon ground cumin

2 generous tablespoons freshly chopped flat leaf parsley, plus extra to garnish

1 small egg, beaten

3 tablespoons fresh white breadcrumbs

1 tablespoon milk

SPICED TOMATO SAUCE

3 tablespoons olive oil

2 onions, finely chopped

3 fat garlic cloves, crushed

1 teaspoon dried oregano

½ teaspoon crushed dried chillies

½ teaspoon ground cumin

200 ml/¾ cup red wine

400-g/14-oz. can chopped tomatoes

1 strip of orange peel

1 teaspoon caster/granulated sugar

sea salt and freshly ground black pepper

SERVES 4–6

Chorizo and olives in red wine with Padrón peppers

Serve this dish alongside the Albóndigas (opposite) and Patatas Bravas (below). Padrón peppers are small, strongly flavoured green peppers that are pan-fried, seasoned with sea salt and eaten whole.

Cut the chorizo into bite-size chunks. Heat a frying pan/skillet over medium heat, add the chorizo and cook until it starts to brown and crisp at the edges. Add the smashed garlic, leaves from the thyme sprig and red wine to the pan and continue to cook over medium heat until the red wine has reduced by half. Add the vinegar and cook for 30 seconds or so. Add the olives and chopped parsley.

Meanwhile, heat the tablespoon of olive oil from the jar of olives in another pan and add the whole Padrón peppers. Cook over medium heat until hot and starting to brown at the edges. Season with salt flakes and serve with the chorizo.

150 g/5 oz. cooking chorizo

1 garlic clove, peeled and smashed

1 sprig of fresh thyme

150 ml/⅔ cup red wine

1 tablespoon sherry vinegar or balsamic vinegar

2 tablespoons mixed olives in olive oil, plus 1 tablespoon oil from the jar

1 tablespoon freshly chopped flat leaf parsley

150 g/5 oz. Padrón peppers, or green (bell) peppers (seeds removed), sliced

sea salt flakes

SERVES 4

Patatas bravas

It's impossible to think of tapas without a plate of piquant patatas bravas. This classic recipe is updated with sweet potatoes and cherry tomatoes.

2 large potatoes

2 orange-fleshed sweet potatoes

4 tablespoons olive oil

1 onion, chopped

2 garlic cloves, sliced

1 teaspoon coriander seeds

1 teaspoon cumin seeds

1 teaspoon Spanish smoked paprika

big pinch of crushed dried chillies

150 g/5 oz. cherry tomatoes

sea salt and freshly ground black pepper

freshly chopped flat leaf parsley, to garnish

SERVES 4

Preheat the oven to 225°C (425°F) Gas 7.

Peel and cut the large potatoes into large, bite-size chunks, tip into a saucepan of salted water and bring to the boil. Cook over medium heat for about 5–7 minutes. Drain and leave the potatoes to dry in the colander.

Peel and cut the sweet potato into chunks the same size as the other potatoes and tip into a roasting pan. Add the blanched potatoes, drizzle half the olive oil over them and roast in the preheated oven for about 30 minutes, or until lightly golden and tender.

Meanwhile, heat the remaining olive oil in a frying pan/skillet. Add the onion and cook for 2–3 minutes until tender but not coloured. Add the garlic and spices and cook for another 2 minutes until golden and fragrant. Add the cherry tomatoes to the pan and continue to cook until they start to soften.

Tip the contents of the pan into the roasting dish with the potatoes, season with salt and black pepper, stir to

combine and return to the oven for a further 5 minutes.

Serve warm, garnished with the freshly chopped parsley.

Pissaladière
with Provençal olive relish

You will fall in love with Pissaladière the first time you bite into a slice. The saltiness of the anchovies and sweetness of the caramelized onions with olive relish is sensational.

Begin by making the dough. Place the flour, yeast, thyme and salt in a ceramic bowl, and mix together. Stir in the water and 60 ml/¼ cup of the oil until combined. Cover with a paper towel or clingfilm/plastic wrap and set aside to rise for 2½–3 hours until it doubles in size.

To caramelize the onions, place a large skillet/frying pan over medium–low heat and add the remaining olive oil and the onions. Cook for about 25 minutes, stirring occasionally, until the onions are golden brown and soft. Set aside.

Preheat the oven to 260°C (500°F) Gas 10 or as high as it will go.

Turn the risen dough out onto the prepared baking sheet. Gently press the dough with the palms of your hands, stretching it to the edges of the pan. Spread the onions over the dough and randomly dollop the Provençal Olive Relish on top. Arrange the anchovies and olives evenly on top.

Bake in the preheated oven for about 15–20 minutes, until the dough is golden and crispy. Remove from the oven and slice into portions.

Serve, garnished with sprigs of thyme and a drizzle of olive oil.

375 g/3 cups all-purpose/plain flour

7 g/¼ oz. active dry/fast action yeast

2 tablespoons fresh thyme leaves

½ teaspoon salt

300 ml/1¼ cups warm water

125 ml/½ cup olive oil, plus extra to serve

8 red onions, peeled and thinly sliced

Provençal Olive Relish (see below)

12–14 anchovy fillets

15 pitted black olives

fresh thyme sprigs, to garnish

a baking sheet, greased with olive oil

SERVES 6

Provençal olive relish

This is Provence in a jar! The olives are drenched in oil and spiced with capers and salty anchovies. It works perfectly atop bruschetta, pizzas, crudités, and pickled eggs, or lightly spread on chicken before roasting in the oven.

Place all the ingredients in a food processor and blend until the mixture is almost smooth but still has some texture. Season with pepper.

Pack the relish into a sterilized glass jar and drizzle with a little olive oil to cover the surface. Store in the refrigerator for up to 6 months.

200 g/2 cups pitted Kalamata olives, drained

12 anchovy fillets

40 g/¼ cup capers, drained

grated zest and juice of 1 lemon

60 ml/¼ cup extra virgin olive oil, plus extra to cover

cracked black pepper

sterilized glass jars with airtight lids (see page 4)

MAKES 700 ML/3 CUPS

Summer salads

Fruit and nut couscous with fresh herbs

The method for cooking the couscous here is almost offensively easy, and produces perfect fluffy grains every time. Mixed with a simple blend of fruits, nuts and fresh herbs, it will become a summer staple in your recipe repertoire.

500 g/1 lb. 2 oz. couscous
olive oil, for frying and drizzling
50 g/⅓ cup whole almonds
50 g/⅓ cup whole cashews
50 g/½ cup whole pecans
1 pomegranate
2 tablespoons chopped fresh flat leaf parsley
2 tablespoons chopped fresh mint
2 tablespoons chopped fresh basil
50 g/⅓ cup raisins
50 g/¼ cup dried apricots, chopped
sea salt and freshly ground black pepper

SERVES 6-8

Put the couscous in a serving bowl and add cold water until it is covered by about 2 cm/¾ inch water. Leave until all the water is absorbed (about 10 minutes), then fluff it up with your hands.

Put all the nuts in a pan with a splash of olive oil and toast over medium heat until they are nicely browned. Set aside to cool.

Remove the pomegranate seeds by cutting the fruit in half, holding it over a bowl and bashing the outside with the back of a wooden spoon so that the seeds fall into the bowl.

Stir the herbs, nuts, pomegranate seeds, raisins and dried apricots into the couscous. Add a little olive oil, season with salt and pepper, and serve.

250 g/9 oz. cooking chorizo

150 ml/⅔ cup extra virgin olive oil, plus extra for frying

4 garlic cloves, bashed

500 g/8⅓ cups fresh breadcrumbs

a sprig of fresh rosemary, finely chopped

200 g/7 oz. curly kale

1 x 400-g/14-oz. can cooked kidney beans, drained

sea salt

feta cheese, crumbled, to serve (optional)

SERVES 4–6

Remove the chorizo from its casing and roughly cut it into pieces. Heat a splash of olive oil in a frying pan/skillet, add the chorizo and fry over medium heat for 5 minutes until it has turned deep red. Allow to cool a little, then pulse in a food processor or chop very finely.

For best results, use a wok for the next part. Put the oil and garlic in the wok or high-sided frying pan/skillet and heat over high heat for a few minutes, until the garlic begins to sizzle nicely. Continue to cook until golden brown all over, then remove and discard. Add the breadcrumbs and rosemary to the wok and fry, stirring regularly, until all the oil has been absorbed and the bread is golden and crunchy. Transfer to paper towels (this helps to soak up some of the oil) and sprinkle with a little salt to draw out any excess moisture.

Bring a deep pan of salted water to the boil and add the kale. Cook for 4–5 minutes, then refresh under cold running water. The kale should retain a bit of bite.

Mix together the fried breadcrumbs, chorizo, kale and kidney beans, and serve. You can crumble some feta over the top if you like, but be careful to adjust the seasoning so that it doesn't become too salty.

Fried bread salad

It's vital that you use fresh breadcrumbs for this flavourful salad – pretty much any bread will do, though it's best to avoid ultra-heavy seeded breads. The bread absorbs a lot of oil while frying, so it's important to use a good-quality extra virgin olive oil, and to remember that it isn't the lightest of salads, so go easy on the portion size. It also makes a great side dish with grilled fish.

olive oil, for frying

50 g/½ cup walnuts

1 pomegranate

2 large or 4 small fennel bulbs,
    halved lengthwise and thinly sliced

1 small red onion, thinly sliced

1 firm mango, stoned/pitted and skinned,
    thinly sliced

1 red chilli, thinly sliced

1 tablespoon chopped fresh coriander/cilantro

1 teaspoon fresh lemon thyme leaves

freshly squeezed juice of 1 lime

sea salt and freshly ground black pepper

SERVES 4

Heat a splash of olive oil in a non-stick
frying pan/skillet, add the walnuts and
toast gently until golden brown. Once
they're just right, remove from the pan
and set aside.

Remove the pomegranate seeds by
cutting the fruit in half, holding it over
a bowl and bashing the outside with
the back of a wooden spoon so that
the seeds fall into the bowl.

Mix all the ingredients together, season
with salt and pepper and serve.

Crunchy fennel salad
with pomegranate, mango and walnuts

Fennel is ubiquitous nowadays, as it rightfully should be. This is a
great salad by itself, or as an accompaniment to grilled fish. Don't
be scared to use the whole of the fennel bulb — it adds colour
to the dish. Reserve some of the sprightly leaves for decoration.

Grilled nectarines with buffalo mozzarella, coppa salami and chilli

A great-looking dish that's bound to get 'oohs' and 'aahs' when delivered to the table. It tastes as good as it looks, and is totally foolproof. Don't worry if you don't have the time (or patience) to grill the nectarines — it's the combination of colours and flavours that makes this simple assembly dish such a hit.

4 nectarines
caster/superfine sugar, for sprinkling
8 slices coppa salami (or Parma ham)
250 g/9 oz. buffalo mozzarella, torn
1 mild red chilli/chile, finely chopped
a bunch of fresh basil leaves
3 tablespoons extra virgin olive oil
50 g/2 oz. Parmesan cheese, shaved
sea salt and cracked black pepper
Balsamic Vinaigrette (see page 48), to serve

SERVES 4

Stone/pit the nectarines and cut them into quarters/fourths. Heat a ridged grill pan until smoking hot, sprinkle the nectarine pieces with sugar and cook for a few minutes on each side, until the char-lines show. Remove and allow to cool.

Mix together the nectarines, salami, mozzarella, chilli, basil and olive oil. Season with salt and black pepper.

Arrange on a plate, sprinkle with the shaved Parmesan and Balsamic Vinaigrette, and serve.

Honey-roasted pear, crispy Parma ham and Dolcelatte salad

This is one of those recipes that relies on its simplicity — the ingredients need little to no improvement upon. Sweet, fresh pears with salty Parma ham and rich Dolcelatte cheese on a bed of peppery rocket/arugula. It's just a handful of ingredients but it works so well that you'll be making this day in, day out.

4 pears (any type will do, but make sure they are fairly firm)

2 tablespoons clear honey

50 g/3½ tablespoons butter, melted

6 slices Parma ham

150 g/5 oz. Dolcelatte cheese

150 g/5 oz. wild rocket/arugula

sea salt and freshly ground black pepper

SERVES 4

Preheat the oven to 200°C (400°F) Gas 6.

Core the pears and cut them into eight wedges lengthways. Toss them with the honey and melted butter and season with salt and pepper. Bake them on a non-stick baking sheet for about 15 minutes: you want them to have begun to turn golden and caramelized, but not to have lost their bite. This is why medium-to-firm pears are essential; if they are too ripe they will fall apart in the oven.

Place the Parma ham slices on a wire rack and roast in the oven for 8–10 minutes. Keep a vigilant watch over them, as they can go from pink to black faster than you think. They should be rigid and deeply coloured, but not burnt. Allow to cool on the rack.

Mix together the rocket/arugula, roasted pears and crispy ham. Arrange the Dolcelatte over the salad as best you can — it's a sticky cheese, so it will resist being broken up. If you've had a bad day and can't be bothered to wrestle with an unco-operative dairy product, you can always opt for the more accommodating Roquefort or Stilton. The results are just as good.

Pearl barley, roast pumpkin and green bean salad

Pearl barley is great in salads, as it manages to retain a bit of texture and is a rare white ingredient, which makes it very useful for improving your salad aesthetics. When it comes to green beans in salads, it is absolutely essential that they are cooked correctly, whole with a bit of bite to crunch through in contrast to the soft pumpkin and silky pearl barley.

500 g/1 lb. 2 oz. pumpkin, peeled and cut into 3-cm/1¼-inch cubes

200 g/generous 1 cup pearl barley

olive oil, for roasting

400 g/14 oz. green beans, topped but not tailed

100 g/3½ oz. sundried tomatoes, roughly chopped

20 pitted black olives

1 tablespoon capers

1 red onion, sliced

1 bunch fresh basil, roughly chopped

1 garlic clove, crushed

sea salt and freshly ground black pepper

SERVES 4-6

Preheat the oven to 200°C (400°F) Gas 6. Toss the pumpkin with a little olive oil and sea salt in a roasting pan. Roast for 20–25 minutes, until soft but not disintegrating.

In the meantime, bring a pan of salted water to the boil and cook the pearl barley for 20–30 minutes. It's impossible to give a precise cooking time, as each batch seems to be different (the same seems to apply to dried chickpeas, for some reason). You want the grains to be al dente, but not chalky or overly chewy. When they're ready, drain them and set aside.

For the beans, bring another pan of salted water to the boil and prepare a bowl of iced water. Add the beans and cook for 3–5 minutes. Test them by giving them a bend; you want them to be flexible but still have a nice snap if you push them too far. Once cooked, drain them and drop them immediately into the iced water. This 'refreshing' process will halt the cooking process and help keep the beans perfectly cooked and vibrantly green.

To assemble the salad, mix the pearl barley with the sundried tomatoes, olives, capers, red onion, basil and garlic. Add this to the roast pumpkin and green beans and stir gently until well combined. Drizzle with a little olive oil and serve.

Buffalo mozzarella with peperonata and rosemary ciabatta croûtons

This combination of creamy white mozzarella and robust, oily peperonata is a sight to behold. The only thing the combination lacks is crunch, which is where the ciabatta croutons come in. Break them up and scatter them over the whole of the dish.

2 red (bell) peppers

2 yellow (bell) peppers

2 plum tomatoes

100 ml/⅓ cup fruity extra virgin olive oil

3 garlic cloves, peeled and whole

1 red onion, very finely sliced

2 bay leaves

1 tablespoon red wine vinegar

½ teaspoon fine sea salt

½ teaspoon white sugar

1 tablespoon capers in vinegar, drained

a handful of sweet cherry tomatoes, halved

leaves from a small bunch of fresh basil

a small ciabatta loaf

needles stripped from 2 sprigs of fresh
    rosemary, finely chopped

4 balls fresh buffalo mozzarella, approximately
    150 g/5 oz. each, halved

sea salt and freshly ground black pepper

rocket/arugula leaves, to serve

a handful of toasted pine nuts, to serve

SERVES 6-8

The peperonata takes a while to cook and is best served at room temperature, so you might like to make it in advance.

Quarter the (bell) peppers and remove the stalk, seeds and any of the white pith. Slice them into thin strips about 1 cm/½ inch wide. Quarter the plum tomatoes, remove the seeds and chop the flesh into small cubes.

Heat a deep frying pan/skillet over medium heat. Add the olive oil and garlic. Fry the garlic on both sides until golden brown, then remove from the pan and set aside. Add the red onion and cook, stirring frequently, until it is pale and translucent but not yet brown. Add the peppers, fried garlic and bay leaves. Cover and cook, covered, for 15 minutes or so, until the peppers are soft but still holding their shape.

Remove the lid and add the diced tomatoes, vinegar, salt and sugar. Cook, uncovered, for a further 10 minutes, then add the capers and cherry tomatoes and take off the heat. The residual heat in the peperonata will soften the cherry tomatoes, but not cook them to a mush. Leave to cool, then add the basil and season with salt and pepper.

Preheat the oven to 200°C (400°F) Gas 6. Slice the ciabatta on the diagonal as thinly as you can. Mix the rosemary with a little olive oil and brush it generously over the ciabatta slices. Season with salt and bake on a wire rack for 5–8 minutes, until golden brown and crisp.

Serve the buffalo mozzarella on a bed of rocket/arugula and the peperonata, with the ciabatta croûtons and pine nuts sprinkled over the top.

Roasted butternut squash, beetroot and goats' cheese salad

4 raw beetroot/beets, ideally 2 red and 2 golden

50 ml/¼ cup clear honey

1 medium butternut squash, peeled, deseeded and cut into wedges

olive oil, for roasting

2 sprigs fresh rosemary, chopped

200 g/7 oz. goats' cheese (the log variety works best here)

½ bunch fresh flat leaf parsley, chopped

finely grated zest of 1 unwaxed lemon

50 g/⅔ cup flaked/sliced almonds

sea salt and freshly ground black pepper

baby spinach leaves or rocket/arugula, to serve

an ovenproof roasting pan, greased with olive oil

SERVES 4

This is a solid, chunky salad that can be prepared well in advance. Beware when cooking beetroot/beet, as everything in the vicinity ends up with red on it.

Preheat the oven to 200°C (400°F) Gas 6.

Put the beetroot/beets into a pan with tepid water and bring to the boil. If you're using both the red and golden types, be sure to cook them separately or the gold colour will get cannibalized by the red. Cook them for approximately 45 minutes (the cooking time can vary wildly). Test them by inserting a knife; if the point goes in easily with little or no resistance, remove and drain in a colander. Run cold water over them and peel while still hot, as the skin comes off much more easily this way.

Cut the beetroot/beets into wedges and place them in the oiled roasting pan. Season generously with salt and pepper and drizzle with the honey.

In a separate roasting pan, mix the butternut squash with a splash of olive oil and the rosemary, and season with salt and pepper.

Put the beetroot/beets and butternut squash in the oven and roast for 45 minutes, or until golden brown. Remove and allow them to cool until you can handle them.

Remove the rind from the goats' cheese and crumble it. Mix the roasted vegetables with the parsley, goats' cheese, lemon zest and almonds. Serve on a bed of baby spinach or rocket/arugula.

315 g/1½ cups white quinoa

360 ml/1½ cups vegetable stock

300 ml/1¼ cups water

1 avocado

40 g/¼ cup segmented and chopped
clementines

45 g/⅓ cup thinly sliced radishes

70 g/⅔ cup watercress, plus extra to serve

45 g/¼ cup pomegranate seeds

40 g/¼ cup pine nuts

8 g/⅛ cup basil leaves

15 g/¼ cup chopped flat leaf parsley

CITRUS DRESSING

6 tablespoons flaxseed oil

2 tablespoons freshly squeezed lemon juice

freshly squeezed juice of 2 clementines

1 teaspoon clear honey

1 teaspoon Dijon mustard

sea salt and freshly ground black pepper

SERVES 4-6

Quinoa salad with spring vegetables and herbs in a citrus dressing

If you want to convert a friend to the wonders of quinoa, try serving this for lunch. There is nothing as enticing as a gorgeous quinoa salad, which looks almost too pretty to eat.

Put the dry quinoa in a large saucepan or pot with the vegetable stock and water over a medium–high heat. Bring to the boil then lower the heat, cover and simmer for 20 minutes. Remove from the heat, fluff with a fork, cover once more and let it sit for another 5 minutes. Remove the lid and set aside to cool.

Prepare the remaining salad ingredients. Chop the avocado and clementines into bite-size pieces and finely slice the radishes. Mix them all together in a separate bowl with the watercress, pomegranate seeds and pine nuts. Gently roll and finely chop the basil and flat leaf parsley then add to the mix.

For the dressing, whisk together the flaxseed oil, lemon and clementine juices, honey and Dijon mustard. Season with salt and pepper to taste.

Mix the quinoa with the bowl of vegetables and seeds and drizzle the dressing on top.

Serve on individual plates with extra watercress and dressing to the side, if desired.

Wild rocket, pomegranate and squash salad with a balsamic dressing

Simple ingredients that pack a punch with flavour, that is what this salad is all about. The sweetness of the butternut squash works well with the heat from the spices.

Preheat the oven to 200°C (400°F) Gas 6.

Discard the seeds and stringy bits from the butternut squash (but leave the skin on). Slice the halves into long strips about 8 mm/⅜ inch thick. Arrange on a baking sheet.

In a pestle and mortar, roughly grind the chilli flakes/hot pepper flakes and spice seeds together, then sprinkle them evenly over the butternut squash. Drizzle a really good glug of olive oil over and season well with salt and pepper. Pop in the preheated oven and roast for about 25–30 minutes, until the edges are just browning and the squash is squishy and cooked but not dried out. Leave to cool.

Toss the rocket/arugula leaves, pomegranate seeds and mint leaves together. Transfer to a serving plate and arrange the squash on top.

To make the Balsamic Vinaigrette, pour the balsamic vinegar into a pan and bring to the boil. Reduce by half then transfer to a sterilized glass jar. Add the remaining ingredients with a pinch of salt, close the jar and shake to combine. Drizzle over the salad just before serving.

1 large butternut squash, halved lengthways

a drizzle of olive oil

1 tablespoon dried chilli flakes/hot pepper flakes (optional)

2 tablespoons coriander seeds

2 tablespoons cumin seeds

sea salt and ground black pepper

200 g/7 oz. rocket/arugula leaves, washed and dried

seeds from 1 large pomegranate (save the juice) or 150 g/5½ oz. pre-packed pomegranate seeds

a handful of fresh mint leaves, stalks removed

BALSAMIC VINAIGRETTE

125 ml/½ cup balsamic vinegar

125 ml/½ cup olive oil

1 teaspoon clear honey

1 teaspoon Dijon mustard

freshly squeezed juice of ½ lemon

a sterilized glass jar with an airtight lid (see page 4)

SERVES 6

2 ripe avocados
2 pink grapefruits
100 g/4 cups rocket/arugula

VINAIGRETTE

1 teaspoon clear honey
3 tablespoons Champagne vinegar
4 tablespoons flaxseed oil
3 tablespoons sunflower seeds
sea salt and freshly ground black pepper

SERVES 4

Prepare the avocados. Using a sharp knife, cut an avocado in half, turning it as you do to cut around the stone. Twist the two halves to separate. Remove the stone and peel the two halves. Repeat with the second avocado then slice the flesh and set aside.

Now prepare the grapefruit. Peel the fruit whole then break into individual segments. Using a sharp knife, carefully score the straight edge of each segment then peel the membrane from the flesh. Repeat until you have released all the deliciously juicy segments.

For the vinaigrette, whisk the honey, Champagne vinegar and flaxseed oil together in a mixing bowl, adding the sunflower seeds at the last minute so as not to damage them. Season to taste.

Place a layer of rocket/arugula on each plate. Arrange the grapefruit and avocado on top, with alternating slices of grapefruit and avocado in concentric semi-circles. You needn't arrange the fruit in this way if you're in a hurry but it looks great when entertaining. Lightly drizzle a line of vinaigrette horizontally across the half-moons of alternating grapefruit and avocado. Enjoy immediately.

Avocado, rocket and grapefruit salad with sunflower seeds

This is a recipe is elegant, simple and classic, with added sunflower seeds and flaxseed oil to boost the omega-3 content. Serve as a light lunch or appetizer in the summer months.

750 g/1½ lb. Jersey Royal new potatoes, washed and left whole

750 g/1½ lb. fresh broad/fava beans, shelled

750 g/1½ lb. fresh peas, shelled

500 g/1 lb. mangetouts/snow peas, trimmed

a bunch of fresh flat leaf parsley, roughly chopped

2 tablespoons chopped fresh mint

180 g/6 oz. cooked ham hock meat, shredded

70 g/2 large handfuls of pea shoots, to garnish (optional)

sea salt and ground black pepper

MUSTARD DRESSING

3 tablespoons extra virgin olive oil

3 tablespoons white wine vinegar

a good pinch of sea salt

1 generous teaspoon French wholegrain mustard

2 teaspoons crème fraîche/sour cream

1 banana shallot (or two small shallots) very finely diced

SERVES 4-6

Ham hock, bean and mint salad with a creamy mustard dressing

Ham hock, broad/fava beans, mint and mustard are a marriage made in flavour heaven. Keep the ham hock, herbs and pea shoots separate from the dressing until just before serving.

Bring a large saucepan of water to the boil, add the new potatoes and boil for 15–20 minutes until cooked through. Remove from the heat, drain and let cool.

Add more water to the pan, bring to the boil again, then add the broad/fava beans and, after 1 minute, add the peas and mangetouts/snow peas. Boil for a further 1 minute before draining, then transfer to a bowl of iced water to refresh. Drain all the peas and beans and put to one side.

For the dressing, put the olive oil and white wine vinegar in a large mixing bowl with a good pinch of salt, and beat with a fork to dissolve the salt in the vinegar. Add the mustard, crème fraîche and shallot and mix well again. Pop the mixed peas and beans and the new potatoes in the bowl with the dressing and mix well.

Just before serving, add the parsley, mint and ham hock to the dressed peas and beans, and toss together. Season to taste with sea salt and ground black pepper, then sprinkle the pea shoots on top, to garnish, if using.

Sweet chilli noodle salad
with crunchy Asian greens

This dish is simple, fresh, extremely tasty and healthy. The sweet chilli jam/sweet chili jelly (below) can also be used with some other recipes in this book. If you haven't got time to make the jam/jelly, store-bought sweet chilli/chili sauce works just as well. This salad is also delicious with king prawns/jumbo shrimp or langoustines added with the noodles and cooked until pink.

3 nests of medium egg noodles

2 whole pak choi/bok choi, leaves separated

1 bunch of asparagus

50 g/2 oz. mangetouts/snow peas

6 spring onions/scallions, sliced

grated zest and freshly squeezed juiced of 1 lime

1 teaspoon palm sugar/jaggery or brown sugar

1 tablespoon fish sauce

5 tablespoons Sweet Chilli Jam (see below)
    or store-bought sweet chilli/chili sauce

a bunch of fresh coriander/cilantro

1 red chilli/chile, finely sliced (optional)

SERVES 4–6

Fill a saucepan three-quarters full with water and bring to the boil. Add your noodles and after 2 minutes put a lidded steamer on top with the pak choi/bok choi, asparagus and mangetouts/snow peas in. (If you do not have a steamer, you can cook these in a separate pan of boiling water.) Cook for a further 2 minutes (so the noodles get 4 minutes, and the greens get 2 minutes in total), then drain them together and blanch them all in cold running water. Drain again, then put both vegetables and noodles into a large mixing bowl along with the spring onions/scallions.

Combine the lime juice and zest, sugar, fish sauce and sweet chilli jam in a small bowl to make a dressing, then fold through the noodles. Garnish with fresh coriander/cilantro and sliced chilli/chile, if using.

Sweet chilli jam

10 red chillies/chiles, roughly chopped

8 red (bell) peppers, deseeded and
    roughly chopped

a 8-cm/3-inch piece fresh root ginger,
    peeled and roughly chopped

8 garlic cloves, peeled

1 x 400-g/14-oz. can cherry tomatoes

750 g/3¾ cups golden caster/raw cane sugar

250 ml/1 cup rice wine vinegar

sterilized glass jars with airtight lids (see page 4)

MAKES 1.6 LITRES/6½ CUPS

Put the chillies/chiles, red (bell) peppers, ginger and garlic into a food processor and whizz together on a pulse setting until the ingredients are finely chopped. (You could do this in a pestle and mortar if you prefer.)

Scrape the mixture out into a saucepan, add the tomatoes, sugar and vinegar and bring to the boil. If any scum gathers at the surface, use a spoon to skim this off before turning down the heat and simmering for 45 minutes. You will need to return to the pan and stir it occasionally so nothing sticks to the bottom. You will see the jam start to turn sticky. Continue to slowly cook for 10–15 minutes, stirring continuously. It should start to look like the inside of a volcano, a thick bubbling lava. Cool slightly before transferring to the sterilized jars and sealing (see Amaretto Cherries, page 133), then let cool to room temperature. Stored in a cool dark place, the jam will keep for up to 3 months but will need to be refrigerated once opened.

Salade Niçoise
with roasted vine tomatoes

The Niçoise salad is an old favourite. It evokes memories of a warm breeze coming off the Mediterranean and sand in between the toes. The colours, vibrant and rich, complement the simple flavours that harmonize perfectly. In Provence they sometimes use artichokes instead of potatoes, so if you're cutting your carbs this is a great alternative.

10 new potatoes, boiled and halved

225 g/½ lb. green beans, trimmed

325 g/¾ lb. vine tomatoes

75 g/½ cup Kalamata olives, pitted

2 tablespoons extra virgin olive oil

5 eggs, at room temperature

1 lemon, halved, for squeezing

4 x 175 g/6 oz. tuna steaks, 2.5 cm/1 inch thick

4 Little Gem/Bibb lettuce hearts, quartered lengthways

12 olive oil-packed anchovies

a large handful of fresh basil leaves (optional)

sea salt and freshly ground black pepper

VINAIGRETTE

a pinch of sea salt

3 tablespoons white wine vinegar

4 tablespoons extra virgin olive oil

1 generous teaspoon Dijon mustard

1 garlic clove, crushed (optional)

SERVES 4-6

Preheat the oven to 200°C (400°F) Gas 6.

Put the new potatoes in a lidded saucepan (preferably with a steaming basket attachment) and bring to the boil. After 10 minutes, add a steamer above the saucepan with the trimmed green beans in. Steam the beans for 4 minutes, then transfer them to a large roasting pan. Add the tomatoes (still on the vine) and olives to the roasting pan and drizzle over the olive oil. Pop the pan in the preheated oven for 12–15 minutes.

Remove the potatoes from the boil (they should have had around 15 minutes total cooking time) and blanch in cold water to cool before draining and halving.

Boil the eggs for 6 minutes, then put the pan under cold running water for a couple of minutes to cool down. When cool, peel the eggs and cut them in half.

Transfer the roasted tomatoes, beans, olives and any warm olive oil to a dish to cool and squeeze over the juice of half a lemon and toss well.

Heat a ridged griddle pan on the hob or over a hot barbecue/outdoor grill for 5 minutes. Brush the tuna steaks with olive oil and season really well with salt and pepper before placing the steaks in the pan. Cook for 3–4 minutes on each side, until the tuna is cooked through.

To make the dressing, add a generous pinch of sea salt to the vinegar and mix to dissolve. Add the olive oil, Dijon mustard and garlic, if using, and mix well.

Lay the lettuce leaves on a large platter and scatter over the new potatoes and anchovies, then add the halved boiled eggs, green beans, roasted tomatoes and olives. You can either choose to keep the tuna steaks whole and place them on the salad, or break them into flaky chunks and toss through. Drizzle the vinaigrette over the salad just before serving, otherwise the leaves can wilt a little. Sprinkle with fresh basil leaves, if using, just before serving.

Lemon, garlic and chilli potato salad

The potato salad is one of those all-time family favourites at any summertime lunch, and this version is no exception. The recipe here uses flavours that are lighter and tastier than a classic mayonnaise version.

1 kg/2¼ lb. new potatoes, unpeeled

100 g/6½ tablespoons butter, softened

2 garlic cloves, crushed

grated zest and freshly squeezed juice of 2 lemons

1 long green chilli/chile, finely diced

a small handful of fresh flat leaf parsley, roughly chopped

a small handful of fresh chives, roughly chopped

sea salt and ground black pepper

SERVES 6

Thoroughly wash the new potatoes under cold running water to remove any dirt, then put them in a large saucepan of water and bring to the boil. Cook for about 15–20 minutes, until the potatoes are tender.

While the potatoes are cooking, put the butter, garlic, lemon juice and chilli/chile in a small bowl and mix well.

Strain the potatoes and transfer them to a large mixing bowl, halving and quartering them as you go. Add the butter mixture to the bowl while the potatoes are still warm and gently stir to coat the potatoes in the butter. When the potatoes have cooled, sprinkle over the lemon zest and fresh herbs, season with salt and a little pepper and mix well again to thoroughly combine.

Lobster and tarragon potato salad

This is a delicate salad perfumed with tarragon that perfectly matches the cooked lobster. It's great for summer eating as an early evening supper before the sun sets.

2 lobsters (about 900 g/2 lbs. each), freshly cooked
680 g/1½ lbs. baby potatoes
1 head frisée or chicory/endive
20 g/1 cup fresh tarragon leaves
2 tablespoons tarragon vinegar
2 tablespoons mayonnaise
1 tablespoon Wholegrain Mustard (see below)
60 ml/¼ cup extra virgin olive oil
sea salt and ground black pepper

SERVES 4

Crack the shell of the lobsters and pull out all the meat. Place in a large bowl and break the meat into large chunks.

Steam the potatoes over a large pot of boiling water for 10–15 minutes, or until a sharp knife easily pierces through them. Rinse the frisée or chicory/endive in cold water and dry it. Tear the leaves and set aside.

In a large serving bowl, whisk together the vinegar, mayonnaise, and mustard. Pour in the olive oil and whisk to combine. Season with salt and pepper.

Add the lobster, warm potatoes, frisée or chicory/endive, and tarragon leaves. Toss together, sprinkle with black pepper, and serve.

Wholegrain mustard

75 g/½ cup yellow mustard seeds
75 g/½ cup brown mustard seeds
235 ml/1 cup red wine vinegar
85 g/¼ cup clear honey
1 garlic clove, finely chopped
a pinch of sea salt

sterilized glass jars with airtight lids (see page 4)

MAKES 475 ML/2 CUPS

Good wholegrain mustards can be hard to find and also a little expensive. This is a really good basic recipe to which you can add wines, spices and herbs. Particularly good on a steak sandwich.

Dry-roast the mustard seeds in a hot pan for 2 minutes. Place the roasted seeds and vinegar in a ceramic bowl and soak overnight.

Put the soaked mustard seeds, honey, and garlic in a food processor and pulse until you have a grainy mustard. Add a little more vinegar if the mix is a little thick. Season with salt.

Pour the mixture into sterilized glass jars and screw the lids on tightly. Store in the refrigerator for up to 2 months.

Sunshine lunches

Gazpacho

This is about as refreshing as it gets. Serve a shot glass of gazpacho on a tapas platter. It's not strictly authentic, but it also doubles up as one hell of a pseudo-Bloody Mary mix.

8 plum tomatoes

1 cucumber

1 red and 1 green (bell) pepper, deseeded and stalk discarded

1 small red onion, peeled

a bunch of fresh basil, chopped

250 ml/1 cup tomato juice

2 tablespoons olive oil, plus extra to serve

sea salt and freshly ground black pepper

a handful of ice, to serve

Tabasco or hot sauce, to serve

SERVES 4–6

Prepare the tomatoes and cucumber by cutting them in half and removing the seeds with a teaspoon. Set the seeds aside, then finely dice the tomato and cucumber flesh and place in a mixing bowl. Dice the (bell) peppers and onion and add to the other vegetables along with the basil. Mix together.

Place about one-third of your diced mixture into a food processor along with the reserved tomato and cucumber seeds, tomato juice and olive oil. Blend until smooth.

Pour the mixture over the remaining diced vegetables and mix together, adding salt and pepper to taste. Refrigerate until nicely chilled.

Serve in individual glasses with a drizzle of olive oil and an ice cube. Put some Tabasco sauce on the table for anyone who wants to add an extra kick.

Minted pea soup with frazzled prosciutto di Parma

Serve this vibrant, zingy soup chilled and in small glasses. It can be prepared and chilled in advance and garnished just before serving.

1 bunch of spring onions/scallions
1 tablespoon olive oil
1 large garlic clove, crushed
1 potato, peeled and diced
750 ml/3 cups hot vegetable stock
300 g/3½ cups frozen peas
a big handful of rocket/arugula, roughly chopped
1 generous tablespoon freshly chopped mint

sea salt and freshly ground black pepper

GARNISHES

4 slices of prosciutto di Parma
1 tablespoon olive oil
pea shoots
crème fraîche or sour cream

SERVES 4–6

Trim and slice the spring onions/scallions. Heat the oil in a medium saucepan, add the spring onions/scallions and garlic and cook over medium heat for a couple of minutes until tender but not coloured. Add the diced potato to the pan along with the vegetable stock. Bring to the boil, then simmer gently for about 20 minutes, or until the potato is really tender. Add the peas, rocket/arugula and mint and cook for a further 3–4 minutes.

Tip the contents of the pan into the bowl of a food processor or blender and blend until smooth. Pass the soup through a fine sieve/strainer and season with salt and black pepper. If the soup is too thick, add a little more vegetable stock.

Chill the soup until ready to serve.

To garnish, roughly tear the prosciutto into pieces. Heat the oil in a frying pan/skillet, add the prosciutto and cook until crisp. Remove from the heat and drain on paper towels.

Divide the soup between 4–6 small glasses. Add a teaspoon of crème fraîche to each, top with pea shoots, crisp prosciutto and a bit of black pepper, and serve immediately.

Cucumber yogurt soup
with chilli and mint salsa

This soup could be considered an acquired taste — but on a warm summer's day it's easy to acquire! It is deliciously refreshing, with a kick from the spicy salsa.

15 g/1 tablespoon butter

4 shallots, diced

2 cucumbers, peeled and deseeded

a small bunch of dill, freshly chopped

leaves from a few sprigs of fresh mint, chopped

a small bunch of chives, freshly snipped

1 slice of white bread

3 tomatoes, peeled, deseeded and diced

400 g/1⅔ cups thick Greek/US strained plain yogurt

200 ml/¾ cup double/heavy cream

1 litre/4 cups vegetable stock

½ teaspoon cumin seeds

½ teaspoon caraway seeds

grated zest of 1 lemon

2 teaspoons Dijon mustard

sea salt and ground black pepper

CHILLI AND MINT SALSA

2 red chillies/chiles, finely diced

a squeeze of fresh lemon juice

a drizzle of olive oil

SERVES 6–8

In a small frying pan/skillet, melt the butter and sauté the shallots for a few minutes, until softened, then leave to cool.

Cut a small chunk from one of the cucumbers and set aside to use in the salsa, along with a little of each of the chopped herbs.

Put the shallots and all the other soup ingredients in a blender and whizz until smooth – the soup should be the consistency of double/heavy cream. The herbs need to be a balance of all three – although the mint will be fairly dominant in the overall freshness and flavour of the soup – so taste and add more of any herb that may be lacking. Season to taste with salt and black pepper, then put the soup in the refrigerator to chill for at least 1 hour before serving.

To make the salsa, finely dice the reserved cucumber. Combine it with the red chillies/chiles and reserved herbs. Mix with a little lemon juice and olive oil to bind, then chill until needed.

Serve the soup in small chilled glasses with a teaspoon, and garnish with the pretty chilli and mint salsa.

5 spring onions/scallions

5 ripe avocados, peeled, stoned/pitted and diced

2 garlic cloves, crushed

2 green chillies/chiles, sliced

½ cucumber, peeled, deseeded and diced

60 g/¼ cup cream cheese

60 g/¼ cup sour cream

1 litre/4 cups vegetable or chicken stock

5 slices of smoked salmon, cut into fine ribbons and any brown meat removed

a small bunch of chives, freshly snipped

a squeeze of fresh lime juice, to taste

sea salt and freshly ground black pepper

GARNISH

a small bunch of fresh coriander/cilantro, chopped

grated zest and freshly squeezed juice of 1 lime

2 tablespoons olive oil

4 ripe tomatoes, peeled, deseeded and finely diced

½ red onion, finely diced

¼ cucumber, finely diced

SERVES 6–8

Trim the greens from the spring onions/scallions and set them aside for the salsa. Roughly chop the spring onion/scallion whites and put them in the bowl of a food processor along with the avocado, garlic, green chillies/chiles, cucumber, cream cheese, sour cream and about one-quarter of the stock to loosen. Blitz on full speed until smooth.

Pour into a large bowl and stir in the remaining stock slowly, to achieve a good, even consistency – it should not be too thin, but should coat the back of a spoon. Avocados vary and the soup's consistency will depend on their fatty or more watery nature, so you may not need to add all of the stock.

Chilled smoked salmon, avocado and chive soup

This is a lovely way to enjoy avocado in the summer and a real treat for lunch with hot crusty garlic bread.

Season the soup with salt and pepper and add the smoked salmon (reserve a few ribbons to garnish), the finely snipped chives and a good squeeze of fresh lime juice. Cover the soup and chill.

To make the salsa garnish, finely chop the reserved spring onion/scallion greens, then put them in a mixing bowl with all the salsa ingredients and mix together gently.

Serve a generous amount of avocado soup with a lovely spoonful of salsa piled in the centre and a few of the reserved salmon ribbons to garnish.

Green summer soup

75 g/5 tablespoons butter

1 onion, diced

1 potato, peeled and diced

4 celery sticks, sliced

1 leek, white part only, sliced

1.5 litres/6 cups vegetable or chicken stock

2 courgettes/zucchini, diced

200 g/1½ cups skinned, fresh baby broad/fava beans

250 g/1¾ cups fresh baby peas

leaves from 2 sprigs of tarragon, freshly chopped

a bunch of chervil, freshly chopped

a large bunch of baby spinach

a bunch of rocket/arugula

200 ml/¾ cup double/heavy cream (optional)

sea salt and ground black pepper

SERVES 6

The base of this soup needs soft vegetables that are happily puréed, but any green vegetable can be added, as long as they are not too tough. The cream is optional, but delicious if added.

Melt the butter in a large saucepan and add the onion, potato, celery and leek. Cook for a few minutes, until beginning to soften, then pour over the stock. Bring the liquid to a simmer and cook for about 15–20 minutes, until the vegetables are tender. Add the courgette/zucchini, beans, peas and herbs to the soup, bring it back to a simmer and cook for 2–3 minutes, then add the spinach and rocket/arugula and remove from the heat. Blend the soup with a stick blender until smooth, then season with salt and pepper. Stir in the cream, if using, ladle the soup into bowls and serve.

Fresh spinach soup
with minted pea and coriander

30 g/2 tablespoons butter

1 onion, diced

2 small potatoes, peeled and diced

800 ml/3⅓ cups vegetable stock

300 g/2 generous cups fresh or frozen peas

400 g/14 oz. spinach leaves, any large stalks removed and roughly chopped if large leaves

8–10 fresh mint leaves

2 tablespoons freshly chopped coriander/cilantro

150 ml/⅔ cup double/heavy cream and sour cream combined (for a little more 'edge' use all sour cream, or for a richer soup use all double/heavy cream)

sea salt and freshly ground black pepper

slow-roasted cherry tomatoes, to garnish (optional)

SERVES 4–6

This is a wow of a soup — as green as the summer fields and as fresh as a handful of herbs!

Melt the butter in a large saucepan set over gentle heat and add the onion and potatoes. Cook for a few minutes, until the butter has been absorbed and the onion has softened, then pour in the stock and simmer for about 15 minutes, until the potatoes are tender. Add the peas and simmer for a further couple of minutes, until they are just soft, being very careful not to overcook them — it is crucial to keep the peas as green as you can. When the peas are tender, add the fresh spinach and immediately draw the pan off the heat. Blend the soup with a stick blender until almost smooth, then add the fresh herbs and continue to blend until silky smooth. Stir in the double/heavy and sour cream and season to taste with salt and pepper.

Ladle the soup into bowls and top with a few slow-roasted cherry tomatoes, if using, for a wonderful sweet and dramatic finish.

Citrus broth with chilli, ginger and king prawns

3 tablespoons peanut/groundnut oil

500 g/1 lb. 2 oz. raw king prawns/jumbo shrimp, shelled

3 garlic cloves, finely sliced

1 tablespoon very finely sliced fresh ginger

1 green chilli/chile, finely diced

1 red chilli/chile, finely diced

250 g/9 oz. straw or mixed exotic Chinese mushrooms, finely sliced

2 fresh kaffir lime leaves

10 spring onions/scallions, whites and greens separated, sliced

4–5 tablespoons fish sauce

1–2 tablespoons soy sauce

freshly squeezed juice of 1 lime

a small bunch of fresh coriander/cilantro, leaves only

200 g/7 oz. mangetouts/snow peas or sugar snap peas, sliced on the angle

sea salt and ground black pepper

lime wedges, to serve

BROTH

2 litres/quarts chicken or fish stock

6 lemongrass stalks, bashed to release their flavour

2 red chillies/chiles, split

6 fresh kaffir lime leaves

1 tablespoon sliced fresh ginger

8 spring onions/scallions, sliced

SERVES 6

With such a fresh and healthy broth, it almost does you good just to read the recipe! It will give you a glow in your cheeks and leave you feeling energized and ready to go. If you can't find straw mushrooms, use shiitake or other Chinese mushroom.

To make the broth, put all the broth ingredients in a large saucepan and bring the liquid to a simmer. Continue to simmer for 15 minutes or so with the pan covered, until an aromatic infusion has been achieved, then pass the broth through a sieve/strainer to remove the seasonings. Set the broth aside until required.

Heat the oil in a large saucepan and add the prawns/shrimp along with the garlic, ginger, green and red chillies/chiles and mushrooms. Toss around until all are well coated in the oil and cook for about 3–5 minutes, until the prawns/shrimp are beginning to turn pink. Pour over the broth, then add the lime leaves, spring onion/scallion whites, fish sauce and soy sauce, and simmer for a further 3–5 minutes.

Add most of the lime juice, taste and then add more lime juice or soy sauce if you feel the seasoning is not sufficient. When happy with the flavour – the soup should be hot, salty and sour – stir in the coriander/cilantro, spring onion/scallion and mangetouts/snow peas or sugar snap peas.

Ladle generous servings of the broth into bowls and serve with lime wedges on the side.

Caramelized pork bánh mì baguettes

A bánh mì is an eclectic mix of classical European ingredients — pork, pâté and baguette — with exotic Asian influences, including herbs, pickled vegetables and soy sauce. There are quite a few elements to this recipe but the end result is totally worth the effort.

300 g/10 oz. pork fillet/tenderloin
1½ tablespoons fish sauce
1 tablespoon honey
½ tablespoon brown sugar
1 tablespoon soy sauce, plus extra to serve
¼ teaspoon sesame oil
1 garlic clove, crushed
1 teaspoon minced ginger
a pinch of ground black pepper
2 large slices baguette
pork liver pâté, to taste
a handful of lettuce leaves
a bunch of fresh coriander/cilantro
a bunch of fresh mint (optional)
red chilli/chile, finely sliced

PICKLED VEGETABLES

4 tablespoons caster/granulated sugar
¾ teaspoon salt
4 tablespoons rice wine vinegar
1 cucumber, halved and sliced thinly
1 carrot, very thinly sliced
½ mooli/daikon, thinly sliced
2 shallots, diced
1 green chilli/chile, sliced

MAKES 2

To make the pickled vegetables, put the sugar and salt in a saucepan with 4 tablespoons water and heat gently until boiling, stirring until the sugar has dissolved and a syrup has formed. Add the rice wine vinegar and leave to cool.

In a small bowl, cover the cucumber, carrot, mooli/daikon, shallots and chilli/chile with the syrup mixture and leave in the refrigerator for up to 3 hours before using. (You only use the vegetables in the sandwich, not the syrup.)

Slice the loin of pork into about 5 mm–1 cm/¼–½ inch thick pieces, put in a bowl and marinate with the fish sauce, honey, brown sugar, soy sauce, sesame oil, garlic, ginger and a pinch of black pepper. Mix really well and leave in the refrigerator for 30 minutes for the flavours to infuse.

Either on a barbecue/outdoor grill or in a very hot griddle pan, cook the pork slices for 2 minutes on each side until charred and caramelized, then leave to cool.

Slice open your baguette, splash soy sauce onto the inside and spread some pork liver pâté along one half. Place the pork slices on top along with the lettuce, pickled vegetables, a good handful of coriander/cilantro and mint, if using, and a sprinkling of sliced chilli/chile.

6 rashers/slices streaky/fatty bacon

2 tablespoons mayonnaise

2 tablespoons fresh tarragon, roughly chopped

freshly squeezed juice and finely grated zest
   of 1 lemon

1 beef/beefsteak tomato, sliced

1 Little Gem/Bibb lettuce, washed

2 bread rolls (toasted brioche rolls work well,
   as do soft white rolls)

sea salt and freshly ground black pepper

LOBSTER

330 g/11 oz. lobster meat
   (1 large rock lobster tail is best)

1 bay leaf

a twist of lemon peel

MAKES 2

The lobster BLT

This divine recipe sticks with the sandwich theme — and what is the best sandwich on the planet? A BLT sub with added flaky lobster and a tangy mayo!

If you need to cook the lobster tail, simply cut down each side of the shell and peel it back to reveal the meat. Put 500 ml/ 2 cups of water in a large saucepan and bring to a simmer. Add the bay leaf, salt and pepper and a twist of lemon peel. Gently place the lobster tail in the water and cook over a low heat for 5–8 minutes. Keep a close eye on it and when the meat turns from translucent to opaque it is cooked. Remove the lobster from the water and let cool.

Heat a grill/broiler and cook the bacon until crisp and golden. Let cool.

In a bowl, combine the mayonnaise with the tarragon and lemon juice and zest.

When the lobster meat is at room temperature, roughly chop it and mix it into the mayonnaise, reserving a little mayo to spread on the rolls.

Split your rolls and toast the inside, then gently spread a little of the reserved lemon mayo over the toasted surfaces, as if you were buttering.

Take the bottom halves of the rolls and start layering up the sandwiches, first adding lettuce leaves, then tomato slices (sprinkle a little salt and pepper over the tomato for seasoning). Spoon half of the lobster mayonnaise into each roll and lay 3 slices of bacon on top. Pop the top half of the roll on and devour.

Asparagus and salmon frittata

This is a wonderful dish that uses fresh, seasonal produce, great for using up asparagus when it is in season. The crunchier the asparagus the better. You can find hot smoked salmon fillets in most supermarkets, but if you can't find them, a poached salmon fillet works just as well, or you could also try this recipe with smoked trout for a different flavour combination.

200 g/7 oz. trimmed asparagus

6 large eggs

2 tablespoons cream cheese

finely grated zest and freshly squeezed juice of 1 lemon

150 g/5½ oz. hot smoked salmon, broken into bite-sized chunks

a handful of chopped fresh dill (or parsley, if you prefer)

2 shallots, diced

olive oil, for frying

sea salt and freshly ground black pepper

a 23-cm/9-inch ovenproof frying pan/skillet

SERVES 6

Bring a pan of salted water to the boil and blanch the asparagus for about 1½–2 minutes, until just tender. Drain, then immediately plunge the asparagus into iced water to refresh. Drain again and leave to dry.

In a large mixing bowl, combine the eggs, cream cheese, lemon zest and juice, salt and black pepper. Stir in the salmon, most of the herbs, and the blanched asparagus.

Preheat a grill/broiler to high.

Heat a little olive oil in a frying pan/skillet set over a medium heat. Add the shallots and sauté until translucent, but do not brown. Pour the frittata mixture over the shallots and make sure the asparagus is evenly distributed and lying flat in the pan. Cook for about 4–5 minutes.

Drizzle a little olive oil over the top of the frittata, then transfer the frying pan/skillet to under the hot grill/broiler and cook for a further 4–5 minutes, until golden on top and puffed around the sides. Remove from the heat and allow to cool before running a spatula around the edge of the frittata and removing from the pan. Slice into wedges to serve.

Mozzarella puttanesca sandwich

Combining mozzarella with this intense, punchy italian sauce is a match made in heaven. Puttanesca's origins are rather humble, created from the last remaining ingredients at the end of an evening's service in the kitchen of a famous Ischian restaurant.

large round or square focaccia,
    halved lengthways and widthways

extra virgin olive oil

4 tablespoons black olive paste

2 tablespoons sun-dried tomato paste

4–6 tablespoons passata/strained tomatoes

2 mozzarella balls, drained and thinly sliced

2 teaspoons dried oregano

2 tablespoons grated/shredded Parmesan

2–3 tablespoons capers, drained

a pinch of dried chilli flakes/hot pepper flakes

a few fresh basil leaves, torn

SERVES 2–4

Brush the outsides of the focaccia halves with olive oil and arrange oil-side down on a clean work surface or chopping board.

Spread two of the non-oiled sides generously with the olive paste. Spread the other two non-oiled sides with the sun-dried tomato paste, then top with the passata. Divide the mozzarella slices between the tomato-coated sides. Sprinkle over the oregano, Parmesan, capers and chilli/hot red pepper flakes. Scatter over a few basil leaves. Top with the olive oil-coated bread, oiled side up.

Without turning the heat on, place the two sandwiches in a large, non-stick frying pan/skillet. If you can only fit one sandwich in your pan, you'll need to cook one sandwich at a time. Turn the heat to medium and cook the first side for 4–5 minutes, then carefully turn with a large spatula and cook the other side for 2–3 minutes, pressing down gently with the spatula until golden brown all over.

Remove from the frying pan/skillet, transfer to a wooden chopping board or a plate and cut the sandwiches in half. Let cool for a few minutes before serving.

Most of the ingredients used here are pantry staples, making this sandwich simple to throw together. It's quicker to make than a pizza but packed full of classic Italian flavours — perfect when you need something tasty in a hurry.

Artichoke, olive and Provolone grilled sandwich

unsalted butter, melted

4 slices panini bread

1–2 tablespoons sun-dried tomato paste

180 g/6 oz. Provolone, grated/shredded or thinly sliced

6–8 marinated artichokes, drained and sliced

65 g/½ cup pitted/stoned green olives, coarsely chopped

½ teaspoon dried oregano

SERVES 2

Brush melted butter on the bread slices on one side. Spread two of the slices with sun-dried tomato paste on the non-buttered side and set aside. Divide the cheese into two equal portions.

Assemble the sandwiches in a large, non-stick griddle pan or a panini grill/press if you have one. Put two slices of bread in the griddle pan, butter-side down. If you can only fit one slice in your pan/skillet, cook one sandwich at a time. Top each slice with half of one of the cheese portions. Arrange half the artichokes on top and sprinkle with half of the olives and oregano. Sprinkle over

the remaining half-portion of cheese and cover with another bread slice, tomato side down.

Turn the heat to medium and cook the first side for 3–5 minutes until deep golden, pressing gently with a spatula.

Carefully turn the sandwich over with a large spatula and cook on the other side for 2–3 minutes more, or until deep golden brown all over.

Remove from the pan, transfer to a plate and cut into quarters. Let cool for a few minutes before serving. Repeat for the remaining sandwich if necessary.

Frittata Lorraine

This little number is a pastry-free alternative to traditional quiche Lorraine. Light, tasty and perfect to take on a picnic.

8 rashers/slices smoked streaky/fatty bacon
1 small shallot, finely diced
1 teaspoon olive oil
8 eggs
200 ml/¾ cup crème fraîche or sour cream
75 g/¾ cup grated/shredded Gruyère cheese
sea salt and ground black pepper

a 20 x 28-cm/8 x 11-inch roasting pan

SERVES 6

Preheat the oven to 180°C (350°F) Gas 4.

Scrunch a sheet of baking parchment into a ball and then flatten it out (this will make it more malleable) and use to line the roasting pan.

Put the bacon in a large frying pan/skillet with the shallots and the olive oil and cook over a medium heat. Stir occasionally until golden and beginning to crisp up.

In a large jug/pitcher or bowl, whisk together the eggs and crème fraîche, then stir in the bacon, shallots and any fat from the pan. Add most of the Gruyère and season well with salt and pepper.

Pour the mixture into the prepared pan, sprinkle with the remaining Gruyère and bake in the preheated oven for 30–35 minutes until golden and set. You can eat it warm, or leave to cool, slice into wedges and pack into a cool box.

Courgette and vintage Cheddar quiche

Late-summer courgettes, lemon and a really strong pungent Cheddar cheese, encased in flaky wholemeal pastry: take this quiche on a picnic and you and your fellow picnickers will be walking on sunshine, whatever the weather!

100 g/¾ cup wholemeal/whole-wheat flour, plus extra for dusting

75 g/⅔ cup plain/all-purpose flour

50 g/3 tablespoons butter, cubed

50 g/3 tablespoons lard, cubed

a pinch of salt

1 egg yolk

FILLING

1 tablespoon butter

1 large white onion, diced

2 courgettes/zucchini, sliced diagonally

175 g/6 oz. mature vintage Cheddar/sharp farmhouse Cheddar, grated

3 eggs

200 ml/¾ cup crème fraîche or sour cream

200 ml/¾ cup double/heavy cream

freshly squeezed juice and grated zest of 1 lemon

a 23-cm/9-inch loose-based tart pan, greased

SERVES 6-8

For the pastry, sift the flours into a large mixing bowl and make a well in the middle. Into the well go the butter, lard and a pinch of salt. Gently rub the flour, butter and lard together with your fingertips until the mixture resembles breadcrumbs, then add 3–4 teaspoons of water and the egg yolk. Bring the mixture together until it is smooth and formed into a ball. (You could do this in a processor if you wish.) Wrap the pastry in clingfilm/plastic wrap and chill in the fridge for at least 30 minutes.

Preheat the oven to 200°C (400°F) Gas 6.

On a floured surface, roll out the pastry thinly to a rough circle and use it to line the prepared tart pan. Cut off any excess overhang, prick the base with a fork, then chill for 10 minutes. Line the chilled pastry case with baking parchment, fill with baking beans and bake in the preheated oven for 15 minutes. Remove the parchment and beans, then cook for a further 4–5 minutes, until the pastry is golden. Lower the oven temperature to 190°C (375°F) Gas 5.

For the filling, melt the butter in a large heavy-based frying pan/skillet and sauté the onion and courgettes/zucchini. When golden, spread over the pastry case and sprinkle over a good handful of grated Cheddar.

In a large mixing bowl, beat the eggs, crème fraîche, cream, and lemon juice and zest together, then stir in most of the remaining cheese (leaving enough to sprinkle over the top of the quiche). Pour the creamy filling over the courgettes/zucchini, right to the top of the pastry case, then sprinkle over any remaining cheese. Bake in the oven for 35 minutes, until the top is soft set and golden brown. Allow the quiche to cool before slicing into wedges to serve.

6 thick slices from a log of Chèvre goats' cheese

6 sprigs of fresh thyme

PASTRY

3 small sprigs of fresh thyme, stalks removed

160 g/1¼ cups plain/all-purpose flour, plus extra for dusting

40 g/3 tablespoons butter

40 g/3½ tablespoons lard

CARAMELIZED ONIONS

3 large red onions, finely sliced

55 g/4 tablespoons butter

40 g/3 tablespoons soft brown sugar

2 tablespoons balsamic vinegar

3 tablespoons cassis liqueur

sea salt and ground black pepper

6 x 10-cm/4-inch loose-based tartlet pans, greased

SERVES 6

Goats' cheese, thyme and red onion tartlets

Caramelized red onion and goats' cheese are one of those flavour marriages made in heaven. Add rich golden pastry and fragrant thyme to the mix and you have a delicious tart that's scrummy to eat at home with a baby leaf salad, or as part of a gourmet on-the-go picnic.

To make the pastry, put the thyme leaves, flour, butter and lard in a food processor and mix on the pulse setting until you have a breadcrumb consistency. Gradually add about 2–3 tablespoons of water to form a soft dough. You now have a lovely thyme pastry. Remove from the food processor, wrap in clingfilm/plastic wrap and leave it in the refrigerator to chill for 30 minutes.

While you are waiting for the pastry to chill, you can prepare the caramelized onions. Pop the red onions, butter, sugar, balsamic vinegar, cassis and seasoning into a large frying pan/skillet and cook over a very low heat. Watch carefully as the caramelizing process starts and the liquid starts to thicken and bubble, as it may burn. Stir the onions occasionally to prevent clumping. Continue to simmer until nearly all of the liquid has evaporated and it is a sticky jam-like consistency.

Now preheat the oven to 200°C (400°F) Gas 6 and place a large baking sheet in there to heat up.

Take your pastry out of the refrigerator and divide it into 6 equal portions. On a floured surface, roll out a portion to a circle 5 mm/¼ inch thick and use it to line one of the prepared tartlet pans, trimming away the excess pastry around the edge. Repeat to line all 6 tartlet pans, then line the pastry with baking

parchment and baking beans. Place the tartlet pans on the hot baking sheet and bake in the preheated oven for about 10 minutes. Remove the beans and lining paper and return to the oven for 5 minutes, then leave the pastry crusts to cool for a few minutes in the pans. Leave the oven on.

Divide the caramelized red onion jam between the tartlets and place a slice of goats' cheese on top, followed by a twist of salt and pepper and a sprig of thyme for decoration. Return to the oven for about 10–15 minutes, or until the top of the goats' cheese is bubbling and tinged with brown. Leave the tartlets to cool before serving or packing into airtight boxes for a picnic.

Salad jars

These recipes bring different components together to create a kaleidoscope of colours that looks very inviting.

2 large beef/beefsteak tomatoes

2 tablespoons olive oil

freshly squeezed juice of ½ lemon

5 carrots

500 g/1 lb. raw beetroot/beets

2 large oranges

1 recipe of Cucumber, Pineapple and Dill Salad (see right)

1 recipe of Herby Citrus Quinoa (see right)

90 g/3 oz. rocket/arugula leaves

2 tablespoons sunflower seeds

sea salt and freshly ground black pepper

sterilized glass jars with airtight lids (see page 4)

SERVES 6

Slice the beef tomatoes into 1 cm/½ inch thick slices. Discard the top and tail ends so you have even slices. Lay the slices flat on a large dish, sprinkle generously with salt and pepper and drizzle with olive oil and a squeeze of lemon juice.

Grate the carrots and then, separately, the beetroot/beets. Lastly, peel and segment the oranges.

You are now ready to build your jars. Spoon 2–3 tablespoons grated beetroot/beets into the bottom of each jar, then lay 3 segments of orange over the top. Next, spoon in 2–3 tablespoons Cucumber, Pineapple and Dill Salad and gently press it down so it evens out. Place a slice of tomato into the jar, reserving the oil and lemon dressing from the tomato plate to use later.

Go for about 4–5 tablespoons of the Herby Citrus Quinoa next, followed by 2–3 tablespoons of grated carrot, then a good handful of rocket/arugula leaves and a sprinkling of sunflower seeds on top. Drizzle with the remaining olive oil and lemon dressing and seal the jar lids.

Cucumber, Pineapple and Dill Salad

1 cucumber

1 x 432 g/15 oz. can pineapple chunks in natural juice, drained

6 sprigs of fresh dill

sea salt and ground black pepper

SERVES 6

Top and tail the cucumber and peel if it is thick-skinned. Now chop it lengthways and then lengthways again so it is quartered. Dice down the cucumber strips in 1-cm/½-inch rows until it is cut into small pieces, then transfer them to a mixing bowl, along with the drained pineapple chunks and mix together.

Roughly chop the dill leaves, discarding any tough stalks, and sprinkle over the salad. Season lightly with salt and pepper and give it a final mix so all the ingredients are well combined.

Herby Citrus Quinoa

300 g/1½ cups quinoa

a handful of basil, freshly chopped

a handful of flat leaf parsley, freshly chopped

a small handful of fresh mint, finely chopped

2 garlic cloves, crushed

1 tablespoon capers, drained

freshly squeezed juice of 1 lemon

2 tablespoons olive oil

150 g/5½ oz. feta cheese, crumbled

sea salt and ground black pepper

SERVES 6

Rinse the quinoa in a sieve/strainer under cold running water, then transfer to a saucepan. Cover the quinoa with boiling water until it is just covered and set the saucepan over a medium heat. Cook for about 15–20 minutes, until the grains are tender, then drain well and leave to cool in a mixing bowl. Using the leaves of the herbs only, put the herbs, garlic and capers into a food processor and chop on a pulse setting. Add the lemon juice and olive oil and season with salt and pepper and pulse once or twice more. Crumble the feta over the cooled quinoa and pour over the herby mixture.

Rustic chicken liver pâté
with toasted baguette and cornichons

This is an adaptation of a classic Tuscan recipe, commonly found served on toasted bread as part of an antipasti platter. It will keep in the fridge for a good few days once covered with oil.

Heat a large pan over a medium-low heat. Add the olive oil, onion and garlic. Cook for about 10 minutes, until the onion is soft and translucent.

Increase the heat to medium–high. Add the chicken livers, anchovies and thyme, along with a good amount of salt (liver needs bold seasoning). Cook for about 10 minutes, stirring frequently. The aim is keep the livers a little pink on the inside, as this will give your pâté a lovely, vibrant hue.

Once cooked, remove the livers from the pan with a slotted spoon and set aside.

Add the capers, brandy and chicken stock to the pan. Bring to the boil and reduce by half.

Place the chicken livers and cooking liquid in the bowl of a food processor and blitz quickly. For a rustic texture, just pulse it quickly. Alternatively, you can blend it until smooth if you prefer. If the mixture seems too dry, just drizzle in a little olive oil while the blade is spinning until you achieve the desired consistency.

Taste and add more seasoning if necessary. Serve with toasted baguette, cornichons and your favourite chutney.

30 ml/2 tablespoons olive oil
1 red onion, diced
1 garlic clove, diced
500 g/1 lb. 2 oz. chicken livers
2 anchovy fillets, chopped
1 teaspoon chopped fresh thyme
2 tablespoons capers
2 tablespoons brandy
2 tablespoons chicken stock/broth
sea salt and freshly ground black pepper
baguette, sliced and toasted, to serve
cornichons and chutney, to serve

SERVES 6-8

Potted crab with melba toast

Seafood has long been known to be a food of love, and potted crab is no exception! Perhaps it's the buttery goodness that harmonizes with the creamy crab and the fiery paprika? Melba toast works wonderfully to add just the right amount of crunch and texture.

Melt a knob/pat of the butter in a frying pan/skillet set over low heat and add the chopped shallot. Very gently, sweat down the shallot until it is translucent but not brown. Let cool.

In a mixing bowl, combine the crab meat, lemon juice, a little grated zest, the paprika and a good pinch of salt and pepper. Once the shallot has cooled, stir it into the crab mixture and divide between the ramekins.

Using the same pan you sweated the shallot in, melt the remaining butter very gently. Once runny, pour the butter over the crab to cover in a thin layer. As the butter sets, press a few parsley leaves in flat. Pop the ramekins in the refrigerator for a few hours to set.

For the melba toast, first turn on your grill/broiler and toast the pieces of bread lightly on both sides. Remove from the heat and cut away the crusts with a sharp knife. With the bread flat on a work surface, slice the bread in half horizonally,

sliding the knife between the toasted edges, and open up the slice like a book. Cut each piece into 4 triangles, then pop them back under the grill/broiler, un-toasted side up, to brown slightly and curl up. Allow to cool before serving.

75 g/5 tablespoons unsalted butter

1 shallot, finely diced

200 g/7 oz. crab meat (white and brown)

freshly squeezed juice and finely grated zest of ½ lemon

a good pinch of paprika or cayenne pepper

1 tablespoon fresh parsley leaves

2–4 slices medium-sliced white bread

sea salt and freshly ground black pepper

SERVES 2

Hand-risen pork pies

All hail the traditional British pork pie! The flaky pastry and meaty filling, along with that delicious flavoured jelly, is one of things that makes Britain great. Making your own pork pies is as easy as 1-2-3, but try to allow yourself a couple of days to complete all the elements.

Firstly, chop the pork shoulder very coarsely into 5-mm/¼-inch chunks. Put them in a large mixing bowl with all the other filling ingredients and mix well. Leave this in the refrigerator overnight to let all the lovely flavours combine.

For the pastry, sift the flour into a large mixing bowl and add the salt. Gently heat the milk and 50 ml/3½ tablespoons water in a saucepan and add the cubes of lard. When the lard has melted, increase the heat and bring to the boil. Take off the heat as the first bubbles appear and slowly pour over the flour, mixing everything together with a wooden spoon until it forms a firm dough.

Knead the dough on a lightly floured surface for around 5–8 minutes, then remove one-third (which will be used to make the pie lids). The remaining dough should be cut into 6 equal portions and shaped into patties. Wrap all the pastry in clingfilm/plastic wrap and chill in the refrigerator overnight.

When you come to make the pies, preheat the oven to 220°C (425°F) Gas 7.

Cover the jam jar in clingfilm/plastic wrap and gently push the jar down into one of the dough patties – this should raise the dough up and around the jar. Gently mould the pastry up the sides to about 4 cm/1½ inches high. (You could also use a pie dolly for this.) Use the cling film/plastic wrap to help you gently remove the jar from the pastry cup. Follow this method with the remaining pieces of dough to make 6 pastry cups, then divide the filling mixture evenly between them.

On a floured surface, roll out the pastry reserved for the lids to about 5 mm/¼ inch thick and cut out 6 rounds using the pastry cutter. Using a pastry brush, paint some egg yolk around the top of the pastry cups and on the inside of a lid and gently press the lid down onto the pies. Use your finger and thumb to gently crimp the sides of the wall and lid together all the way around, making sure the pastry is sealed completely or the pie may collapse in the oven. Give each pie an egg wash (not the crimp though), then make a hole in the centre of the lid for the steam to escape and to be able to pour the jelly in later when the pies are cooked.

Place the pies on a baking sheet and bake in the preheated oven for about 1¼ hours until a rich, deep golden brown. Leave to cool on a wire rack.

For the jelly, put the pig's trotter, bouquet garni, carrot and celery stalk in a large saucepan with 5 litres/quarts of water and bring to the boil, then simmer for about 4 hours. Allow the water to evaporate down to about 500 ml/2 cups, but do not let the pan boil dry – top it up with more water if necessary. After 4 hours, strain the liquid stock into a measuring jug/cup – you will need 500 ml/2 cups. Dissolve the gelatine in the warm stock, continuously stirring until it thickens. It is now ready to fill the pies.

Insert a funnel into the hole in the lid of one of the pies (you may have to re-open this with a skewer) and slowly pour the jelly mixture into the hole until it just overflows. Repeat with the remaining 5 pies, then leave them, preferably overnight, to cool in a fridge. Eat cold with a teaspoon of Branston pickle.

FILLING

400 g/14 oz. boneless pork shoulder

110 g/4 oz. bacon lardons/very thickly sliced bacon, cut into cubes

2 sprigs of thyme, leaves only, finely chopped

1 sprig of sage, leaves only, finely chopped

½ teaspoon anchovy sauce (such as Geo Watkins)

a pinch of ground nutmeg

½ teaspoon ground mace

sea salt and freshly ground black pepper

PASTRY

340 g/2⅔ cups strong plain bread flour, plus extra for dusting

a good pinch of salt

40 ml/3 tablespoons milk

120 g/½ cup lard, cubed

1 large/US extra-large egg yolk, beaten, to glaze

JELLY

1 pig's trotter

1 bouquet garni

1 carrot

1 celery stalk

5 sheets of leaf gelatine/1 envelope powdered gelatine

Branston pickle, to serve

sterilized glass jar with an airtight lid (see page 4)

an 8-cm/3¼-inch round pastry cutter

SERVES 6

Grilled halloumi cheese and Mediterranean vegetable stack

Roasted vegetables and halloumi are a wonderful amalgamation of tastes and textures, but be careful not to overcook the halloumi as it can become a little rubbery and squeaky.

1 large aubergine/eggplant

3 small courgettes/zucchini, any colour

1 large red onion

2 red (bell) peppers

3–4 tablespoons olive oil

3 large sprigs of rosemary

freshly squeezed juice of ½ lemon

2 x 250-g/9-oz. blocks of halloumi cheese, sliced

sea salt and freshly ground black pepper

cocktail sticks/toothpicks

SERVES 6

Preheat the oven to 220°C (425°F) Gas 7.

Slice the aubergine/eggplant and the courgettes/zucchini widthways into 1 cm/½ inch thick slices. Peel and chop the onion into ⅛th wedges. Lastly, chop the red (bell) peppers in half, remove the seeds and cut into 1 cm/½ inch thick strips. Drizzle a little olive oil on a baking sheet and arrange the vegetables with the rosemary sprigs on top. Drizzle over more olive oil, making sure there is plenty on the aubergine/eggplant slices as they tend to dry out in the oven, and season very well with salt and pepper. Roast in the preheated oven for 30–40 minutes, until the vegetables are tender and lightly browned on the outside. Leave to cool before squeezing the lemon juice lightly over all of the vegetables.

Brush a griddle pan with olive oil and set over a medium–high heat. Cut the halloumi lengthways into around 6 slices per block and cook on the griddle for 30 seconds on each side until lightly golden lines appear.

To assemble, start with a slice of the halloumi cheese on the bottom and layer up your vegetables and 1 further slice of halloumi per stack. Secure with cocktail sticks/toothpicks to keep the stacks together, but remember to remove them before serving!

Polenta tart with goat's cheese and tomatoes

It's easy to forget that corn has its place as a grain. There are rougher cuts of corn as a grain, known as polenta, with some of the bran layer in tact which count as a wholegrain.

1 litre/4 cups water
170 g/1 cup polenta/cornmeal
1 tablespoon butter (optional)
1 teaspoon sea salt
1 teaspoon freshly ground black pepper

TOPPING

300 g/1 cup cherry tomatoes
1½ teaspoons sea salt
1½ teaspoons freshly ground black pepper
1 tablespoon olive oil
150 g/6 oz. goats' cheese
a handful of fresh basil leaves, to garnish

a baking sheet, greased

SERVES 4-6

For the topping, cut the tomatoes in half and mix together with the salt, pepper and olive oil. Set aside.

Preheat the oven to 180°C (350°F) Gas 4.

Bring the water to the boil in a large saucepan or pot, then slowly pour in the polenta while whisking. Whisk for five minutes until fully combined. Reduce the heat, then cover and cook for 15 minutes, stirring vigorously every 5 minutes. Remove the lid, then add a tablespoon of butter, if desired, and the salt and pepper. Stir together, then pour onto the prepared baking sheet and bake in the preheated oven for 20 minutes.

Remove from the oven and allow to cool completely before cutting into square portions of equal size.

Put some of the tomato topping on each square and sprinkle with a little goats' cheese. Garnish with torn fresh basil and season with a little extra salt and pepper, then serve immediately.

Best-ever barbecue

Veg antipasto

2 red (bell) peppers

4 baby fennel bulbs, trimmed, fronds reserved

1 large aubergine/eggplant

1 red onion

2 large courgettes/zucchini

a few fresh herb leaves, such as basil and dill

extra virgin olive oil, to taste

freshly squeezed lemon juice, to taste

sea salt and freshly ground black pepper

crusty bread or grilled polenta, to serve

HERB MARINADE

2 sprigs of rosemary

2 sprigs of thyme

4 bay leaves

2 large garlic cloves, coarsely chopped

pared zest of 1 unwaxed lemon

1 teaspoon cracked black peppercorns

230 ml/1 cup extra virgin olive oil

SERVES 4

Serving a large platter of grilled vegetables provides a lovely start to any barbecue party. A delicious way to serve them is on a bed of grilled polenta or accompanied by some fresh, crusty bread.

Cut the (bell) peppers into quarters and discard the seeds. Cut the fennel into 5-mm/¼-inch slices. Cut the aubergine/eggplant into thick slices and cut in half again. Cut the onion into wedges and cut the courgettes/zucchini into thick slices.

To make the marinade, strip the rosemary and thyme leaves from the stalks and put in a mortar. Add the bay leaves, garlic and lemon zest and pound with a pestle to release the aromas. Put the mixture in a bowl and add the peppercorns and olive oil.

Put all the vegetables in a large bowl, pour over the marinade, and toss gently until evenly coated. Cover and let marinate in a cool place for at least 1 hour.

Preheat the barbecue/outdoor grill or stovetop grill pan until hot, add the vegetables and cook until they are all tender and lightly charred. Let cool, then peel the (bell) peppers.

Sprinkle the vegetables with the herbs, reserved fennel fronds, olive oil, and lemon juice, then season lightly.

Grilled artichokes with chilli-lime mayonnaise

Try to find small or baby artichokes for this dish so that they can be cooked without any blanching first.

18 small artichokes
1 lemon, cut in half
2 tablespoons extra virgin olive oil
sea salt and freshly ground black pepper
lime wedges, to serve

CHILLI-LIME MAYONNAISE

1 dried chipotle chilli/chile
2 egg yolks
300 ml/1¼ cups olive oil
freshly squeezed juice of 1 lime

SERVES 6

To make the mayonnaise, cover the chipotle with boiling water and let soak for 30 minutes. Drain and pat dry, then cut in half and scrape out the seeds.

Finely chop the chilli/chile flesh and put in a food processor. Add the egg yolks and a little salt and blend briefly until frothy. With the blade running, gradually pour the oil through the funnel until the sauce is thick and glossy. Add the lime juice and, if the mayonnaise is too thick, 1 tablespoon warm water. Taste and adjust the seasoning with salt and pepper, if necessary, then cover and set aside.

Trim the stalks from the artichokes and cut off the top 2.5 cm/1 inch of the globes. Halve the globes lengthways, cutting out the central 'choke' if necessary. Rub the cut surfaces with lemon juice to stop them discolouring.

Toss the artichokes with the oil and a little salt and pepper. Cook over medium-hot coals or on a preheated stovetop grill pan for 15–20 minutes, depending on size, until charred and tender, turning halfway through the cooking time. Serve with the mayonnaise and wedges of lime.

Grilled corn with chilli-salt rub

6 corn cobs, husks removed

2 tablespoons extra virgin olive oil, plus extra to serve

3 ancho chillies/chiles

30 g/1½ tablespoons sea salt, plus extra for cooking the corn

3 limes, cut into wedges

SERVES 6

One of the American Southwest's most popular chillies/chiles is the ancho, the dried version of the poblano. When ground to a fine powder, it has a smoky flavour and is mild to medium on the heat scale — delicious with the sweet, nutty taste of corn.

Trim the ends of the corn. Bring a large saucepan of lightly salted water to the boil, add the corn, and boil for 1–2 minutes. Drain and refresh under cold water. Pat dry with paper towels.

Preheat a barbecue/outdoor grill or stovetop grill pan until hot. Brush the corn with oil and cook for 5–7 minutes, turning frequently until charred all over.

Meanwhile, remove the stalks and seeds from the ancho chillies/chiles. Chop the flesh coarsely and, using a spice grinder or mortar and pestle, grind to a powder. Transfer to a small bowl, then mix in the salt.

Rub the lime wedges vigorously over the corn, sprinkle with the chilli/chile salt and serve with extra oil for drizzling.

Just the ticket for people who don't eat meat but love a good burger. The onion pickle can be made ahead and kept in the refrigerator for several days.

Mushroom burgers with chilli mayonnaise and onion pickle

1 fresh hot red chilli/chile, about 5 cm/2 inches long, seeded and chopped

about 120 ml/½ cup mayonnaise

2 tablespoons extra virgin olive oil

4 large portobello mushrooms, stems trimmed

4 hamburger buns, split in half

salad leaves

sea salt and freshly ground black pepper

ONION PICKLE

2 tablespoons olive oil

2 red onions, thinly sliced

60 ml/¼ cup redcurrant jelly

1 tablespoon red wine vinegar

SERVES 4

To make the onion pickle, heat the oil in a saucepan, add the onions, and sauté gently for 15 minutes or until very soft.

Add a pinch of salt, the redcurrant jelly, vinegar, and 2 tablespoons water and cook for 15 minutes more, or until the mixture is glossy with a jam-like consistency. Let cool.

Preheat a barbecue/outdoor grill or stovetop grill pan, then cook the chilli/chile whole for 1–2 minutes, or until the skin is charred and blackened. Transfer to a sealable plastic bag, seal and let cool slightly. Peel the chilli/chile, then remove and discard the seeds. Chop the flesh and transfer to a food processor. Add

the mayonnaise and process until the sauce is speckled red. Taste and adjust the seasoning with salt and pepper, if necessary.

Brush the olive oil over the mushrooms, season well with salt and pepper, and cook on the barbecue/outdoor or grill pan, stem-side down, for 5 minutes. Using a spatula, flip the mushrooms and cook them on the other side for about 5 minutes, until they are tender.

Toast the split buns for a few minutes on the barbecue/outdoor grill or grill pan, then fill them with the mushrooms, salad leaves, onion pickle and a spoonful of the mayonnaise.

Grilled sardines with gremolata and toasted breadcrumbs

A fantastically simple dish that hits all the right notes — smoky, succulent meat, lightened by the refreshing lemon and parsley combination, with breadcrumbs adding that bit of crunch. It's ideal barbecue/cook-out food that can feed hundreds for next to no cost. It goes perfectly with a simple salad, or on a thick slice of grilled sourdough bread.

8 medium sardines, scaled and gutted

sea salt and freshly ground black pepper

lemon wedges, to serve

a handful of rocket/arugula leaves, to serve

BREADCRUMBS

2 thick slices of white sourdough bread

2 garlic cloves, bashed

a pinch of pine nuts

1 tablespoon extra virgin olive oil

a few sprigs of fresh rosemary, chopped

a few sprigs of fresh thyme, chopped

GREMOLATA

a handful of fresh flat leaf parsley, roughly chopped

finely grated zest of 1 unwaxed lemon

1 garlic clove, finely grated

50 ml/scant ¼ cup/3 tablespoons extra virgin olive oil

SERVES 4

Start by preparing your breadcrumbs (it's a good idea to do these ahead of time so you can leave them to dry out and become extra crunchy). Tear the bread into pieces and put in a food processor. Blend until you have a rough, uneven consistency, then set aside. If in doubt, play it safe and keep the pieces big — the last thing you want is a fine powder that will turn into sludge when you try to toast it.

For the gremolata, mix together the parsley, lemon zest and garlic, add the oil and allow the flavours to infuse.

Pour a thin layer of oil over the base of a non-stick frying pan/skillet that's big enough to hold all the breadcrumbs comfortably in a single layer. Add the garlic cloves and set it over a high heat. Remove the garlic once it begins to turn brown. Add the breadcrumbs, pine nuts and chopped herbs. Cook, stirring, so that the crumbs don't catch and burn. Once they have turned a lovely, crunchy golden brown, tip them out onto paper towels and sprinkle generously with salt (this will help them dry out). These breadcrumbs are pretty versatile and can be used as a form of seasoning for all kinds of dishes, such as grilled/broiled salmon, or on salads to add a bit of bite — whatever takes your fancy. They're also great mixed with grated Parmesan cheese and loaded onto your favourite pasta.

Get your barbecue/outdoor grill or stove-top grill pan heating to smoking hot. Season the sardines liberally with salt and gently place them on the grill horizontally. They shouldn't need any oil as there's enough in the skin already. They will take about 3–5 minutes on each side, depending on the heat. The secret to cooking fish on a grill is not to force it. If it's sticking and doesn't want to be turned, that's because it isn't ready to be turned, so leave it for a minute more before turning.

Sprinkle the fish with the gremolata and toasted breadcrumbs and serve with rocket/arugula and a wedge of lemon.

Grilled fish bathed in oregano and lemon

This recipe brings the tastes and aromas of beach-side Greek tavernas to the home kitchen. This is a typical Mediterranean dish of char-grilled bream with oil, oregano, and garlic, but you could use other small fish such as snapper, or even trout, if you prefer. This dish is perfect for alfresco cooking.

2 unwaxed lemons
240 ml/1 cup extra virgin olive oil
1 tablespoon dried oregano
2 garlic cloves, finely chopped
2 tablespoons chopped fresh flat leaf parsley
6 snapper or bream, well cleaned and scaled
sea salt and freshly ground black pepper

SERVES 6

Grate the zest of 1 lemon into a small bowl and squeeze in the juice. Add 180 ml/¾ cup of the oil, the oregano, garlic, parsley, salt and pepper. Let infuse for at least 1 hour.

Wash and dry the fish inside and out. Using a sharp knife, cut several slashes into each side. Squeeze the juice from the remaining lemon into a bowl, add the remaining 60 ml/¼ cup oil, salt and pepper and rub the mixture all over the fish.

Heat the flat plate of a barbecue/outdoor grill for 10 minutes, add the fish, and cook for 3–4 minutes on each side until charred and cooked through. Alternatively, use a stovetop grill pan or large, heavy frying pan/skillet. Transfer to a warm platter, pour over the dressing, and let rest for about 5 minutes before serving.

Grilled mackerel, orange, fennel and red onion salad with tapenade

Fish can often be a tough customer to pair up with other foods, and its delicate flavour is all too often swamped by what surrounds it. Not mackerel, though: it's in the heavyweight category, alongside red mullet and a few other choice bruisers. This recipe is a veritable slug-fest of flavours, each one vying for top spot with equal promise. Tarragon is one of the few herbs that seems to divide opinion, so feel free to swap it for basil if you're not a fan.

2 oranges
4 bulbs fennel
1 red onion
1 small bunch fresh flat leaf parsley, roughly chopped
1 sprig fresh tarragon or dill, roughly chopped
8 large mackerel fillets
sea salt and freshly ground black pepper

TAPENADE

250 g/9 oz. black olives (ideally Kalamata), pitted
1 garlic clove, peeled
30 g/¼ cup pine nuts
½ small bunch fresh basil
½ small bunch fresh flat leaf parsley

1 teaspoon dark navy rum
4 tablespoons olive oil
freshly squeezed juice of ½ lemon
3 tablespoons capers
3 anchovy fillets

VINAIGRETTE

100 ml/⅓ cup olive oil
freshly squeezed juice of ½ lemon
a pinch of sugar

SERVES 6-8

For the tapenade, put all the ingredients in a food processor and pulse until amalgamated into a rough paste. Add a little extra oil to loosen it if the blades aren't catching everything. Set aside.

Meanwhile, prepare the oranges for the salad by cutting the skin off to reveal the flesh underneath. Using a sharp knife, carefully cut out each segment between the membranes so that you have a little wedge of pure orange with no white pith. You should end up with nice clean segments and a star-shaped central core of pith. Squeeze the central core to extract any juice and set aside to use in the vinaigrette.

Slice the fennel and red onion as thinly as possible. Mix together the orange segments, fennel, red onion, parsley and tarragon.

Preheat a ridged stove-top grill pan or barbecue/outdoor grill. Put all the vinaigrette ingredients, along with the reserved orange juice, in a jar and shake it to emulsify.

Season the mackerel fillets with salt and pepper, sprinkling a little extra on the skin side to help release the oils during cooking. Gently place them on the hot grill and cook for around 5 minutes, or until they can be turned over easily. Finish cooking on the other side.

Dress the salad with the vinaigrette and put the mackerel fillets on top. Spoon a little tapenade onto each fillet and serve.

Hot-smoked Creole salmon

Smoking food on the barbecue/outdoor grill is simply magical – the flavours are truly wonderful. You will need a barbecue/outdoor grill with a lid for this recipe. If you have a gas grill, follow the manufacturer's instructions for indirect grill-smoking.

4 salmon fillets, skinned, about
    225 g/8 oz. each
sea salt and freshly ground black pepper

CREOLE RUB

½ small onion, finely chopped
1 garlic clove, finely chopped
1 tablespoon freshly chopped thyme
1 tablespoon paprika
1 teaspoon ground cumin
1 teaspoon sea salt
¼ teaspoon cayenne pepper
1 tablespoon brown sugar

MANGO AND
SESAME SALSA

1 large ripe mango, peeled, stoned/pitted
    and chopped
4 spring onions/scallions, chopped
1 hot red chilli/chile, seeded and chopped
1 garlic clove, crushed
1 tablespoon light soy sauce
1 tablespoon freshly squeezed lime juice
1 teaspoon sesame oil
6 g/½ tablespoon sugar
1 tablespoon chopped fresh coriander/cilantro

a large handful of wood chips, such as hickory,
    soaked in water for 1 hour, drained

SERVES 4

To make the Creole Rub, put all the ingredients in a small bowl and stir well.

Wash the salmon under cold running water and pat dry with paper towels. Using tweezers, pull out any bones.

Put the fish in a dish and work the Creole rub all over it. Cover and place in the refrigerator for at least 1 hour.

For the mango and sesame salsa, put the chopped mango in a bowl and add the spring onions/scallions, chilli/chile, garlic, soy sauce, lime juice, sesame oil, sugar, coriander/cilantro, salt and pepper. Mix well and let stand for 30 minutes.

Preheat a charcoal barbecue/outdoor grill. When the coals are hot, rake them into 2 piles at either side of the grill and put a foil drip tray in the middle. Tip half the soaked wood chips onto each pile of coals. Cover with the lid, keeping any air vents open during cooking. As soon as the wood chips start to smoke, put the salmon fillets in the centre of the grill, cover and cook for 15–20 minutes, until the salmon is cooked.

To test the fish, press the salmon with your finger – the flesh should feel firm and start to open into flakes. Serve hot or cold with the mango and sesame salsa.

Peppered tuna steak with salsa rossa

Salsa rossa is one of those divine Italian sauces that transforms simple meat and fish dishes into food nirvana. The slight sweetness from the peppers is a good foil for the spicy peppercorn crust.

60 g/⅓ cup mixed peppercorns,
   coarsely crushed

6 tuna steaks, 225 g/8 oz. each

1 tablespoon extra virgin olive oil

mixed salad leaves, to serve

SALSA ROSSA

1 large red (bell) pepper

1 tablespoon extra virgin olive oil

2 garlic cloves, crushed

2 large ripe tomatoes, peeled and
   coarsely chopped

a pinch of dried chilli flakes/hot pepper flakes

1 tablespoon dried oregano

1 tablespoon red wine vinegar

sea salt and freshly ground black pepper

SERVES 6

To make the salsa rossa, broil the (bell) pepper until charred all over, then put in a plastic bag and let cool. Remove and discard the skin and seeds, reserving any juices, then chop the flesh.

Put the oil in a frying pan/skillet, heat gently, then add the garlic and sauté for 3 minutes. Add the tomatoes, hot red pepper flakes, and oregano, and simmer gently for 15 minutes. Stir in the chopped (bell) peppers and the vinegar, and simmer for 5 minutes to evaporate any excess liquid.

Transfer the mixture to a blender and purée until fairly smooth. Add salt and pepper to taste and let cool. The salsa may be stored in a screw-top jar in the refrigerator for up to 3 days.

Put the crushed peppercorns on a large plate. Brush the tuna steaks with oil, then press the peppercorns into the surface.

Preheat a stovetop grill pan or barbecue/outdoor grill until hot, add the tuna, and cook for 1 minute on each side.

Wrap loosely in foil and let rest for 5 minutes before serving with the salsa rossa and a salad of mixed leaves.

Whole salmon stuffed with herbs

A great way to prepare whole salmon is to remove the central bone, then tie the two fillets back together. If your filleting skills are limited, just ask your fishseller to fillet the fish for you.

1.8 kg/4 lb. whole salmon, filleted

110 g/1 stick butter, softened

30 g/1 cup chopped fresh mixed soft-leaf
   herbs, such as basil, chives, mint, parsley,
   and tarragon

grated zest of 1 unwaxed lemon

1 garlic clove, crushed

sea salt and freshly ground black pepper

olive oil, for brushing

kitchen twine

SERVES 8

Put the salmon fillets flat on a board, flesh-side up. Carefully pull out any remaining bones with tweezers. Put the butter, herbs, lemon zest, garlic and plenty of pepper in a small bowl and beat well. Spread the mixture over one of the salmon fillets and put the second on the top, arranging them top to tail.

Using kitchen twine, tie the fish together at 2.5-cm/1-inch intervals. Brush with a little oil, sprinkle with salt and pepper and cook on the flat plate of a barbecue/outdoor grill for 10 minutes on each side. Remove the salmon from the heat and let rest for 10 minutes. Remove the twine and serve the fish, cut into portions.

Piri-piri squid

Piri-piri, a Portuguese spicy condiment traditionally used to baste chicken, is a combination of chopped red chillies/chiles, olive oil and vinegar. It is generally very hot and only a little is needed to add spice to the food. Here I have tempered the heat, but you can use more chillies/chiles if you like it spicier.

8 medium squid bodies, about 225 g/8 oz. each
freshly squeezed juice of 1 lemon
sea salt
lemon wedges, to serve

PIRI-PIRI SAUCE

8 small red chillies/chiles, such as bird's eye
300 ml/1¼ cups extra virgin olive oil
1 tablespoon white wine vinegar
freshly ground black pepper
16 wooden skewers, soaked in water for 30 minutes

SERVES 4

To prepare the squid, put the squid body on a chopping/cutting board and, using a sharp knife, cut down one side and open the tube out flat. Scrape away any remaining insides and wash and dry well.

Skewer each opened-out body with 2 skewers, running them up the long sides of each piece. Rub a little salt over each one and squeeze over the lemon juice. Let marinate in the refrigerator for 30 minutes.

Meanwhile, to make the piri-piri sauce, finely chop the whole chillies/chiles without seeding them, and transfer to a small jar or bottle with a lid. Add the extra virgin olive oil, vinegar and a little salt and pepper. Shake well to combine, then set aside.

Meanwhile, preheat a barbecue/outdoor grill or stovetop grill pan until hot.

Brush the squid with a small amount of the piri-piri sauce, then cook for 1–1½ minutes on each side, until the squid is nicely charred.

Drizzle with extra piri-piri sauce and serve immediately with lemon wedges.

Scallops cooked in their shells with Thai juices

This dish works brilliantly as an aperitif. After using up energy simply soaking up the sun, these little babies are a scrumptious appetizer before the main event. Scallops are such a luxury, yet they can be inexpensive when bought in season. Look out for scallops that have been harvested by hand-diving, as these are more environmentally sustainable than those that have been dredged from the sea bed. Just a single king scallop or sea scallop is enough to sate an appetite, and the sweet versus salty Thai juices are the icing on the cake. Be very careful — the shells get extremely hot on the barbecue/outdoor grill, so keep fingers away until they are cool enough to handle.

100 ml/⅓ cup rice wine vinegar

100 g/½ cup sugar

⅓ cucumber, finely diced

1 shallot, finely diced

1 small red chilli/chile

½ teaspoon salt

6 large scallops, in their shells

a small handful of fresh coriander/cilantro, chopped

sea salt and freshly ground black pepper

SERVES 6

Put the vinegar, sugar and 60 ml/¼ cup water in a saucepan and bring to the boil, then gently simmer until it is a syrupy consistency, but not too thick. Add more vinegar and a little more sugar if it becomes too gloopy. Let the syrup cool, then add the cucumber, shallot, chilli/chile and salt. Pour the sauce into a lidded jar. It is best to make and use this sauce on the same day, but it doesn't hurt to keep it in the refrigerator or cooler until ready to use.

If the scallops need preparing, use a spoon to remove them from the shell (reserve the shells) and clean thoroughly by removing the frill, the black stomach sack and any other debris. (You could get your fishmonger to do this for you.) You can then put the scallops back in their shells and wrap up well in a layer of baking parchment and then in cling film/plastic wrap. As with all seafood, they must be kept at a very cool

temperature until you are ready to cook them, so make sure they are next to the ice packs and well chilled before grilling. Place 6 shell halves onto a very hot barbecue/outdoor grill or straight onto the burning coals — the hotter the shells get the better. Now season the scallops and place one into each curve of the very hot shells, then place the other 6 shell halves on top to act as a lid. Cook for 3 minutes before turning the shells over and cooking on the other side for a further 2–3 minutes. Remove the shells from the heat and arrange on a serving platter.

Take the top shell lid off all the scallops, gently spoon over some of the Thai sauce and sprinkle over some chopped coriander/cilantro. If you simply can't wait to gobble the scallop down, use a fork to spear the scallop and eat with gusto before waiting for the shell to cool enough to knock the juices back.

Langoustines with harissa mayo

Similar to scampi, langoustines are actually a member of the lobster family. Unfortunately, due to over-fishing they are quite rare, but if you do find them they make a delicious treat. You are more likely to find langoustines already cooked, but if you do find them still alive they should be cooked as soon as possible. If you cannot find langoustines, lobster tails or large tiger prawns/jumbo shrimp make an equally delicious alternative.

24 langoustines
a baguette, to serve

HARISSA MAYO

150 g/⅔ cup mayonnaise
1 garlic clove, crushed
a small handful of fresh mint, finely chopped

2 teaspoons harissa paste
freshly squeezed juice of 2 limes and grated zest of 1 lime

a lobster pick or wooden cocktail sticks/toothpicks

SERVES 6

You are more likely to find cooked langoustines over raw. With this in mind you will need to gently reheat them, but not cook them as this will toughen them up. Simply place them straight onto the outer edge of a hot barbecue/outdoor grill and cook for about 1 minute on one side, then turn them over and cook for 30 seconds on the other side. If you do manage to find raw ones, cook them for 4 minutes on each side.

For the harissa mayo, combine all the ingredients and mix well. Serve a dollop on the side of the langoustines and chunks of bread to mop up the juices.

To eat a langoustine, first break the head and thorax off the langoustine and discard. Peel off the shell around the tail and eat, then crack the claws to get to the juicy meat inside. You may find a lobster pick is useful, but I also find a wooden cocktail stick/toothpick works just as well.

Swordfish is a meaty fish that holds its shape well on the barbecue/outdoor grill. It works well with the bold flavours of aromatic sumac and zesty orange here. You could use other meaty white fish instead.

500 g/18 oz. boned swordfish, cut into bite-sized chunks

2 oranges, cut into wedges

a handful of fresh bay leaves

2–3 teaspoons ground sumac

MARINADE

1 onion, grated

1–2 garlic cloves, crushed

freshly squeezed juice of ½ lemon

2–3 tablespoons olive oil

1–2 teaspoons tomato purée/paste

sea salt and freshly ground black pepper

4 metal skewers or 4–6 wooden skewers, soaked in water before use

SERVES 4

Swordfish kebabs
with oranges and sumac

In a shallow bowl, mix together the ingredients for the marinade. Gently toss the chunks of swordfish in the marinade, cover and set aside to marinate for 30 minutes.

Thread the marinated fish onto the skewers, alternating it with the orange segments and the occasional bay leaf. If there is any marinade left, brush it over the kebabs.

Prepare a barbecue/outdoor grill or stovetop grill pan. Cook the kebabs for 2–3 minutes on each side, until the fish is nicely browned. Sprinkle the kebabs with sumac and serve.

Note Sumac is an increasingly popular spice. It grows wild, but is also cultivated in Italy, Sicily and throughout the Middle East. It is widely used in Lebanese, Syrian, Turkish and Iranian cooking. The red berries have an astringent quality, with a pleasing sour-fruit flavour. They are used whole, but ground sumac is also available from Middle Eastern grocers or specialist online retailers.

900 g/2 lb. monkfish tail, cut into chunks

12–16 cherry tomatoes

1–2 teaspoons smoked paprika

1–2 lemons, cut into wedges

CHERMOULA

2 garlic cloves

1 teaspoon coarse sea salt

1–2 teaspoons cumin seeds, crushed or ground

1 fresh red chilli/chile, deseeded and chopped

freshly squeezed juice of 1 lemon

2 tablespoons olive oil

a small bunch of fresh coriander/cilantro,
    roughly chopped

4–6 metal skewers or 4–6 wooden skewers,
    soaked in water before use

SERVES 4–6

Monkfish kebabs with chermoula

Chermoula is a classic Moroccan flavouring of garlic, chilli/chile, cumin and coriander/cilantro, which is employed as a marinade for fish and chicken tagines and grilled dishes. Any meaty, white fish can be used here but monkfish cooks particularly well over charcoal.

To make the chermoula, use a mortar and pestle to pound the garlic with the salt to a smooth paste. Add the cumin, chilli/chile, lemon juice and olive oil and stir in the coriander/cilantro.

Place the fish chunks in a shallow dish and rub with the chermoula. Cover and chill in the refrigerator for 1–2 hours.

Thread the marinated monkfish and cherry tomatoes alternately onto the skewers. Heat a barbecue/outdoor grill or stovetop grill pan. Cook the kebabs for 2 minutes on each side, or until the monkfish is nicely browned. Dust with a little paprika and serve with wedges of lemon for squeezing over them.

Char-grilled tamarind prawns

500 g/18 oz fresh, large prawns/jumbo shrimp, deveined and trimmed of heads, feelers and legs

MARINADE

3 tablespoons tamarind pulp

250 ml/1 cup warm water

2 tablespoons sweet soy sauce

1 tablespoon sugar

freshly ground black pepper

TO SERVE

leaves from a small bunch of fresh coriander/cilantro

2–4 fresh green chillies/chiles, deseeded and sliced

a packet of wooden or bamboo skewers, soaked in water before use

SERVES 2–4

This is popular street food in Malaysia and Indonesia, where the irresistible aroma emanating from the stalls will make you feel very hungry every time you pass by.

Rinse the prepared prawns/jumbo shrimp well, pat dry and, using a very sharp knife, make an incision along the curve of the tail. Set aside.

Put the tamarind pulp in a bowl and add the warm water. Soak the pulp until soft, squeezing it with your fingers to help dissolve it. Strain the liquid and discard any fibre or seeds. In a bowl, mix together the tamarind juice, soy sauce, sugar and black pepper. Pour it over the prawns/shrimp, rubbing it over the shells and into the incision in the tails. Cover, refrigerate and leave to marinate for about 1 hour.

Insert a soaked wooden skewer into each marinated prawn/jumbo shrimp.

Heat a barbecue/outdoor grill or stovetop grill pan. Cook the prawns/shrimp for about 3 minutes on each side, until the shells have turned orange and the prawns/jumbo shrimp are cooked through, brushing them with the marinade as they cook.

Serve immediately, garnished with the coriander/cilantro leaves and sliced green chillies/chiles.

Rosemary skewered sausages

All hail the banger! A sausage is synonymous with a barbecue/cook-out but this recipe gives it a bit of a kick by infusing the flavours of fresh rosemary right into the heart of every sausage. Most important here is making sure you buy decent sausages, so the flavours don't get lost in bucket-loads of fat. Lastly, make sure you have a baguette to hand to wrap around the sausage — and some decent mustard wouldn't go amiss either!

12 pork sausages of your choice

12 long sprigs of fresh rosemary

1 tablespoon olive oil

chunks of baguette, to serve

French mustard, to serve (optional)

a metal or wooden skewer

SERVES 6

Take a sausage and spear it lengthways with the skewer. Remove the skewer and slowly thread a rosemary branch through where the hole has been made. If the rosemary breaks do not worry, just thread the rest of the sprig into the sausage from the other side.

Repeat this process with the rest of the sausages and rosemary sprigs, then brush them with olive oil. Place the sausages on a hot barbecue/outdoor grill and cook for 10–15 minutes, turning occasionally, until cooked through and browned on all sides.

Serve the sausages in a torn baguette with some good French mustard, if liked, or simply hot off the barbecue/grill.

Indian spice rub

1 teaspoon ground cumin

1 cinnamon stick, broken into pieces

2 tablespoons cardamom pods, bashed

1 teaspoon whole cloves

1 teaspoon ground turmeric

1 teaspoon smoked paprika

1 teaspoon garam masala

MAKES 4 TABLESPOONS/¼ CUP

This spicy rub goes with everything, and adding oil or yogurt turns it into a paste that can be spread under the skin of chicken or on fish. I love to mix up the spices in this basic recipe and change it to Madras or Tandoori.

Heat a cast-iron pan over a medium–high heat and add all the ingredients. Roast for 3–4 minutes, stirring constantly so they don't burn. Transfer the roasted spices to an electric spice grinder and process to a coarse powder.

Store the rub in a glass jar with a tight-fitting lid for up to 6 months.

To use, put the meat in a ceramic dish, sprinkle over the spice rub, and rub it into the meat. Leave to marinate for 8–24 hours in the fridge. Let the meat come to room temperature, then cook according to the recipe on page 99, or as preferred. This spice rub can also be used on beef, fish, and poultry.

Indian-spiced leg of lamb with tandoori breads

Ask your butcher to cut thick lamb steaks from the leg for this recipe. Marinate them overnight for the best results — this way, all these wonderful Indian spices are flavouring the meat. They are great thrown on a barbecue/outdoor grill and then sliced up and tossed onto Indian breads.

2 leg of lamb bone-in steaks (about 900 g/2 lb.), cut 4 cm/1½ inches thick
sea salt and cracked black pepper
3 tablespoons Indian Spice Rub (see opposite)
olive oil, to drizzle

RAITA

240 ml/1 cup Greek/US strained plain yogurt
120 g/1 cup grated/shredded cucumber
1 garlic cloves, finely chopped
a small bunch of fresh mint, stalks removed and leaves torn
sea salt

TO SERVE

Tandoori Indian breads, such as naan
fresh coriander/cilantro, to garnish
lime wedges

SERVES 4

Rinse the lamb under cold water and pat dry with a paper towel. Lay the steaks in a ceramic dish and season with salt and pepper. Sprinkle the Indian Spice Rub over the meat and rub it in, making sure all the meat is coated. Drizzle with a little olive oil, then cover and refrigerate for 8–24 hours.

To make the raita, put all the ingredients in a mixing bowl and mix thoroughly. Cover and refrigerate until you are ready to serve.

Remove the lamb from the fridge and bring to room temperature.

Heat a barbecue/outdoor grill or stovetop grill pan to medium–high. Lay the lamb steaks on the grill and cook for 4–5 minutes each side for medium rare. Cook longer if you prefer your lamb well done. Transfer the steaks to a wooden board, cover and rest for 10 minutes.

While the lamb steaks are resting, grill the tandoori breads until crispy and golden brown. Arrange on a platter.

Slice the lamb into thin strips and pile on top of the breads. Drizzle over the juices and top with spoonfuls of raita. Sprinkle with fresh coriander/cilantro leaves and serve with lime wedges.

450 g/1 lb. chicken fillets

12 lime leaves

a 5-cm/2-inch piece of fresh ginger, peeled and roughly chopped

3 garlic cloves, peeled and roughly chopped

60 ml/¼ cup coconut oil or vegetable oil

grated zest and freshly squeezed juice of 2 limes

1 tablespoon curry powder

1 teaspoon chilli/chili powder

½ teaspoon smoked paprika

10 g/½ cup coriander/cilantro leaves

TO SERVE

lime wedges

Garlic and Mango Madras Relish (see below)

12 wooden skewers, pre-soaked

MAKES 12 SKEWERS

Chicken tikka bites
with garlic and mango madras relish

These tikka bites are especially welcome in the summer. Thrown straight onto the barbecue or grill/broiler, they are ready in minutes. The lime leaves give a delightful floral fragrance to the dish.

Begin by preparing the chicken. Cut the chicken fillets into 3.5-cm/1½-inch chunks. Thread a piece of chicken onto a soaked wooden skewer, then a lime leaf and another piece of chicken. Take another wooden skewer and repeat until you have used up all of the chicken. Place the skewers in a large shallow bowl and set aside.

Put the chopped ginger and garlic, coconut oil, lime zest and juice, curry powder, chilli/chili powder, paprika and coriander/cilantro leaves in a food processor. Blend until smooth.

Pour the curry sauce over the prepared chicken skewers, coating the meat. Cover and set in the refrigerator to marinate for 2–4 hours.

Light the barbecue/outdoor grill or place a grill pan over medium–high heat. Place the skewers directly on the heat or in the grill pan and cook for 4 minutes on each side, until the chicken is cooked through.

Serve with lime wedges and Garlic and Mango Madras Relish.

1 ripe mango, skin and stone/pit removed

1 red chilli/chile, finely diced

grated zest and juice of 1 lime

1 tablespoon grated fresh ginger

2 spring onions/scallions, thinly sliced

1 garlic clove, finely chopped

½ teaspoon Madras curry powder

¼ teaspoon smoked paprika

60 ml/¼ cup rice wine vinegar

1 tablespoon sesame oil

2 tablespoons peanut/groundnut oil

1 tablespoon fish sauce

sea salt, to season

MAKES 350 ML/1½ CUPS (12 OZ.)

Garlic and mango madras relish

Vibrant and gutsy Madras curry powder livens up the mango medley in this quick and versatile relish. Serve with absolutely anything — it's especially good piled on top of fish tacos.

Begin by preparing the mango. Cut the flesh into 5-mm/½-inch cubes and place in a bowl. Add the chilli/chile, lime zest and juice, ginger, spring onions/scallions, garlic, curry powder and paprika. Toss to combine.

In a separate bowl, whisk together the vinegar, sesame oil, peanut/groundnut oil and fish sauce. Pour over the mango mix and stir well to coat. Season with salt and chill in the refrigerator before serving.

Cumin-flavoured lamb kebabs with hot houmous

Typical fodder at the street grills, these kebabs/kabobs are enjoyed throughout the Middle East and North Africa. To prepare them successfully, you will need large metal skewers with wide, flat blades to hold the meat.

500 g/18 oz. finely minced/ground lean lamb

1 onion, grated

2 teaspoons ground cumin

1 teaspoon ground coriander

1 teaspoon paprika

½–1 teaspoon cayenne pepper

1 teaspoon sea salt

a small bunch of fresh flat leaf parsley, finely chopped

a small bunch of fresh coriander/cilantro, finely chopped

HOT HOUMOUS

225 g/7 oz. dried chickpeas, soaked overnight and cooked in plenty of water until tender, or a 400-g/14-oz. can cooked chickpeas, drained

50 ml/3 tablespoons olive oil

freshly squeezed juice of 1 lemon

1 teaspoon cumin seeds

2 tablespoons light tahini

4 tablespoons thick, strained natural yogurt

sea salt and freshly ground black pepper

40 g/3 tablespoons butter

TO SERVE

a leafy herb salad

flatbreads

2 metal skewers with wide, flat blades

SERVES 4–6

Mix the minced/ground lamb with the other ingredients and knead well. Pound the meat to a smooth consistency in a large mortar and pestle, or whizz in a food processor. Leave to sit for an hour to let the flavours mingle.

Meanwhile, make the houmous. Preheat the oven to 200°C (400°F) Gas 6. In a food processor, whizz the chickpeas with the olive oil, lemon juice, cumin seeds, tahini and yogurt. Season to taste, tip the mixture into an ovenproof dish, cover with foil and put in the preheated oven to warm through.

Wet your hands to make the meat mixture easier to handle. Mould portions of the mixture around the skewers, squeezing and flattening it, so it looks like the sheath to the sword.

Prepare a barbecue/outdoor grill or stovetop grill pan. Cook the kebabs for about 4–5 minutes on each side, or until cooked through.

Quickly melt the butter and pour it over the houmous. When the kebabs are cooked on both sides, slip the meat off the skewers, cut into bite-sized pieces and serve with the hot houmous, a leafy herb salad and flatbreads.

Lamb shish kebab
with yogurt and flatbread

This is the ultimate kebab/kabob and a great way of using up day-old bread.

500 g/18 oz. minced/ground lean lamb

2 onions, finely chopped

1 green chilli/chile, finely chopped

4 garlic cloves, crushed

1 teaspoon paprika

1 teaspoon ground sumac

leaves from a small bunch of fresh flat leaf parsley, finely chopped

SAUCE

2 tablespoons olive oil plus a knob/pat of butter

1 onion, finely chopped

2 garlic cloves, finely chopped

1 fresh green chilli/chile, deseeded and finely chopped

400-g/14-oz. can chopped tomatoes

1 teaspoon sugar

sea salt and freshly ground black pepper

TO SERVE

2 tablespoons butter

8 plum tomatoes

1 large pide or plain naan bread, cut into pieces

1 teaspoon ground sumac

1 teaspoon dried oregano

225 g/8 oz. thick, strained natural yogurt

a bunch of flat leaf parsley, freshly chopped

1 large metal skewer with a wide, flat blade, plus 1 long thin skewer

SERVES 4

Put the minced/ground lamb in a bowl. Add all the other kebab/kabob ingredients and knead well, until it resembles a smooth paste and is quite sticky. Cover and chill in the refrigerator for about 15 minutes.

To make the sauce, heat the oil and butter in a heavy-based saucepan. Add the onion, garlic and chilli/chile, and stir until they begin to colour. Add the tomatoes and sugar, and cook, uncovered, until quite thick and saucy. Season to taste, then keep warm.

Wet your hands to make the meat mixture easier to handle. Mould portions of the mixture around the skewer, squeezing and flattening it, so it looks like the sheath to the sword. Thread the tomatoes onto the thin skewer.

Prepare a barbecue/outdoor grill or stovetop grill pan. Cook the kebab for 4–5 minutes on each side, or until cooked through. Add the tomatoes to the grill and cook until charred and soft. While both are cooking, melt the butter in a heavy-based frying pan/skillet, add the pide pieces and toss until golden. Sprinkle with some of the sumac and oregano and arrange on a serving plate. Spoon some sauce and half the yogurt on top.

When the kebab is cooked on both sides, slip the meat off the skewer, cut into pieces and arrange on top of the pide along with the tomatoes. Sprinkle with salt and the remaining sumac and oregano. Add the sauce and yogurt and garnish with parsley.

500 g/18 oz. pork fillet/tenderloin, cut into bite-size cubes or strips

MARINADE

4 shallots, peeled and chopped

4 garlic cloves, peeled

2–3 teaspoons Indian curry powder

2 tablespoons dark soy sauce

2 tablespoons sesame or peanut/groundnut oil

PINEAPPLE SAUCE

4 shallots, peeled and chopped

2 garlic cloves, chopped

4 dried red chillies/chiles, soaked in warm water until soft, seeded and chopped

1 lemongrass stalk, trimmed and chopped

25 g/1 oz fresh ginger, peeled and chopped

2 tablespoons sesame or peanut oil

200 ml/¾ cup coconut milk

2 teaspoons tamarind paste

2 teaspoons sugar

1 small fresh pineapple, peeled, cored and cut into slices

sea salt

short wooden or bamboo skewers, soaked in water before use

SERVES 4

Curried pork satay with pineapple sauce

This spicy satay is popular in Malaysia and Singapore. A combination of Indian, Malay and Chinese traditions, it is best accompanied by a rice pilaf or chunks of bread.

To make the marinade, use a mortar and pestle, or a food processor, to pound the shallots and garlic to form a paste. Stir in the curry powder and soy sauce, and bind with the oil. Rub the marinade into the meat, making sure it is well coated. Cover and refrigerate for at least 2 hours.

In the meantime, prepare the sauce. Using a mortar and pestle, or a food processor, pound the shallots, garlic, chillies, lemongrass and ginger to form a paste. Heat the oil in a heavy-based pan and stir in the paste. Cook for

2–3 minutes until fragrant and beginning to colour, then stir in the coconut milk, tamarind and sugar. Bring the mixture to the boil, then reduce the heat and simmer for about 5 minutes. Season to taste and leave to cool. Using a mortar and pestle, or a food processor, crush 3 slices of the fresh pineapple and beat them into the sauce.

Prepare a barbecue/outdoor grill or stovetop grill pan. Thread the marinated meat onto the prepared skewers. Line them up over the hot charcoal or on the grill pan and place the remaining slices of pineapple beside them.

Char the pineapple slices and chop them into chunks. Cook the meat until just cooked through, roughly 2–3 minutes each side, and serve immediately with the charred pineapple chunks for spearing, and the sauce for dipping.

Fiery beef satay
with peanut sauce

Beef, pork or chicken satays cooked in, or served with, a fiery peanut sauce are hugely popular throughout Southeast Asia. This particular sauce is a great favourite in Thailand, Vietnam and Indonesia. It is best to make your own but commercial brands are available under the banner satay or sate sauce.

500 g/18 oz. beef sirloin, sliced against the grain into bite-size pieces

1 tablespoon groundnut/peanut oil

PEANUT SAUCE

60 ml/2 oz. groundnut/peanut oil or vegetable oil

4–5 garlic cloves, crushed

4–5 dried Serrano chillies/chiles, seeded and ground with a pestle and mortar

1–2 teaspoons curry powder

60 g/2 oz. roasted peanuts, finely ground

TO SERVE

a small bunch of fresh coriander/cilantro

a small bunch of fresh mint

lime wedges

short wooden or bamboo skewers, soaked in water before use

SERVES 4–6

To make the sauce, heat the oil in a heavy-based saucepan and stir in the garlic until it begins to colour. Add the chillies/chiles, curry powder and the peanuts and stir over a gentle heat, until the mixture forms a paste. Remove from the heat and let cool.

Put the beef pieces in a bowl. Beat the groundnut/peanut oil into the sauce and tip the mixture onto the beef. Mix well, so that the beef is evenly coated and thread the meat onto the prepared skewers.

Prepare a barbecue/outdoor grill or stovetop grill pan. Cook the satay sticks for 2–3 minutes on each side, then serve the skewered meat with the fresh herbs to wrap around each tasty morsel.

Classic beef burger
with tomato ketchup and lettuce

Sometimes less is more, and a simple burger made with good-quality beef speaks for itself. Serve simply with ketchup and lettuce in the bun and some fries on the side.

220 g/8 oz. lean minced/ground beef
2 teaspoons tomato purée/paste
1½ tablespoons fresh breadcrumbs
1 teaspoon chopped fresh parsley
1 tablespoon olive or vegetable oil (optional)
a large pinch of sea salt and freshly
　ground black pepper

TO SERVE
2 sesame seeded burger buns
tomato ketchup
a few lettuce leaves

MAKES 2 BURGERS

Put the beef in a bowl with the tomato purée/paste, breadcrumbs, parsley and salt and pepper. Work together with your hands until evenly mixed. Divide the beef mixture in half and shape into two burger patties. Press each burger down to make them nice and flat.

Prepare a barbecue/outdoor grill or stovetop grill pan, or heat the oil in a frying pan/skillet. Cook the burgers over a medium–high heat for 5 minutes on each side, or until cooked through.

Slice the burger buns in half. Spread a spoonful of tomato ketchup on the base of each bun and put the cooked burgers on top. Put a few lettuce leaves on top of each burger and finish with the lids of the buns.

Top dogs

Buy the best hot dogs you can find. Those packed in natural casings are usually very good, especially with the caramelized onions and wholegrain mustard in this recipe.

2 onions, cut into thin wedges

2–3 tablespoons extra virgin olive oil

1 tablespoon freshly chopped sage leaves

4 natural-casing frankfurters
   or bratwursts, pricked

4 hot dog buns

4 tablespoons Wholegrain Mustard
   (see page 55)

2 ripe tomatoes, sliced

sea salt and freshly ground black pepper

SERVES 4

Put the onion wedges in a bowl, add the olive oil, sage, and a little salt and pepper, and mix well. Preheat the flat plate on a barbecue/outdoor grill and cook the onions for 15–20 minutes, stirring occasionally until golden and tender. If you have a charcoal grill, cook the onions in a frying pan/skillet on the grill. Alternatively, cook them on a preheated stovetop grill pan. Keep the onions hot.

Meanwhile, cook the frankfurters or bratwursts for 10–12 minutes, turning frequently until browned and cooked through. Transfer to a plate and let rest.

Cut the buns almost in half, then put on the grill rack or stovetop grill pan and toast for a few minutes. Remove from the heat and spread with mustard. Fill with the tomatoes, sausages and onions, and serve.

Outdoor dining

New England clambake

Simply layer seafood in a large pan for this home clambake. Cover an outside table with newspaper and pour the contents of the pot out. Dig in, armed only with lobster crackers!

Set the stock pot over a medium–high heat. Pour in 240 ml/1 cup water and add the wine, seasoning, salt and garlic, and bring to a boil.

Add the onion and potatoes to the pan, then place the lobsters on top. Cover and cook for 15–20 minutes. Add the clams and corn and continue to cook for a further 8–10 minutes with the lid tightly on. Check to see if the clam shells have opened, if not, continue to cook until they have.

Remove the pan from the heat and carefully strain off the cooking liquid. Tip the remaining contents of the pot

240 ml/1 cup white wine

2½ tablespoons of Homemade Old Bay Seasoning (see below)

1 teaspoon coarse sea salt

4 garlic cloves, bashed

1 red onion, roughly chopped

900 g/2 lb. baby potatoes, halved

2 lobsters, about 680–900 g/1½–2 lb. each

2 dozen Manila clams

4 fresh corn cobs, cut into 4 parts

a small bunch of fresh tarragon or flat leaf parsley, roughly chopped

TO SERVE

225 g/2 sticks butter, melted

crusty bread

3 lemons and 3 limes, cut into wedges

a stock pot or pasta pot with a tight-fitting lid

SERVES 4-6

onto the prepared table or transfer to a large platter. Serve with the melted butter, crusty bread, and lemons and limes to squeeze over.

Homemade Old Bay seasoning

Old Bay Seasoning was created in the 1940s in Baltimore, Maryland, where there is an abundance of seafood, and it's an American classic. Although nobody will ever know what is in the original recipe, this is a quick version that tastes great.

Put all the ingredients into an electric spice grinder and process until you have a fine powder.

Store the seasoning in a glass jar with a tight-fitting lid for up to 6 months.

To use, add 1 or 2 tablespoons to clambakes, steamed crab, fish stews and soups, or use to spice up marinades.

4 whole green cardamom pods

4 dried bay leaves

1 teaspoon yellow mustard powder

1 teaspoon yellow mustard seeds

1 teaspoon celery seeds

1 teaspoon cracked black pepper

1 teaspoon sea salt

1 teaspoon paprika

½ teaspoon whole cloves

½ teaspoon dried garlic powder

½ teaspoon ground nutmeg

½ teaspoon ground allspice

½ teaspoon chilli/chili powder

MAKES 4 TABLESPOONS/¼ CUP

Sardines with Campari, peach and fennel

This dish uses the bitterness of Campari as a foil for the sweetness of peaches and the saltiness of the small fish. The flavours of this dish will transport you straight to the shores of Italy.

6 sardines or 2 mackerel fillets

2 ripe peaches, stoned/pitted

2 tablespoons Campari

3 tablespoons olive oil

1 teaspoon sea salt

1 tablespoon peppercorn-sized breadcrumbs

a handful of rustic croûtons (made by toasting a piece of sourdough and ripping it into small pieces)

1 fennel bulb, cut into thin strips, fennel tops reserved

a handful of fresh mint leaves

1 teaspoon freshly ground black pepper

a handful of black olives, pitted

SERVES 2

If using sardines, butterfly them: remove the heads, trim the fins and slit the fish open from the belly down to the tail. Open the fish like a book and place, skin-side up, on a board. Press down with your hand along the backbone to flatten it. Turn the fish over and pull out the backbone, cutting off the tail. Finally, pick out any obvious bones left behind.

Finely grate one of the peaches into a bowl and add the Campari. Set half of this mixture aside in another bowl. Marinate the fish in half of the mixture for 20 minutes.

Heat a frying pan/skillet over high heat. Add 1 tablespoon of the olive oil, the salt and a layer of breadcrumbs. This will help prevent the flesh of the fish sticking. Cook the fish for 4 minutes on one side, until the flesh is opaque.

Flip and cook for 2 minutes on the other side. Add the croûtons to the pan to toast them further.

Slice the remaining peach into slivers. Mix them with the fennel, croûtons, mint leaves and pepper. Whisk the reserved peach-Campari mixture with the remaining olive oil and sprinkle over the fennel salad. Toss to coat.

Serve the fish fillets on top of the fennel salad. Garnish with fennel tops and black olives.

Cod fillets with lemon and thyme crust on a bean and chorizo stew

This isn't a quick dish, but the results are well worth the effort involved. Prepare the beans a day or two in advance — they'll only get better, and it's one less thing to worry about.

100 g/scant 1½ cups fresh breadcrumbs

leaves from 3–4 sprigs of fresh thyme

grated zest of 1 unwaxed lemon

30 g/¼ cup pine nuts

2 skinless cod fillet pieces, approximately 200 g/7 oz. each, as thick as possible

plain/all-purpose flour, for dusting

2 eggs, lightly beaten

sea salt and freshly ground black pepper

2 lemon wedges, to serve

BEAN STEW

3 tablespoons olive oil

120 g/4½ oz. cooking chorizo, cubed

2 red onions, finely chopped

2 garlic cloves, chopped

1 red (bell) pepper, finely chopped

1 fennel bulb, finely chopped

2 stalks celery, sliced

a sprig of fresh rosemary

1 x 400-g/14-oz. can butter/lima beans

200 ml/¾ cup vegetable stock

SERVES 2

Preheat the oven to 200°C (400°F) Gas 6.

For the bean stew, heat the olive oil in a heavy-based saucepan over a high heat. Fry the chorizo until crisp and its aromatic oil has been released. Remove and set aside for later.

Add the onions, garlic, red (bell) pepper, fennel, celery and rosemary sprig. Fry over medium–high heat, stirring regularly, until the onions are beginning to brown – about 10 minutes.

Add the butter/lima beans and their juice (this helps to thicken up and flavour the stew). Add the stock at the same time. Cook over a high heat for

10 minutes, or until some of the liquid has reduced. Remove from the heat and add the fried chorizo.

Mix the breadcrumbs with the thyme leaves, lemon zest and pine nuts, and season with salt and pepper.

Get three bowls ready. Add some flour to one, the eggs to another, and the breadcrumbs to the last one.

Press one side of the cod fillet into the flour, then the eggs, and finally the breadcrumbs. Push it down firmly so that as many breadcrumbs as possible stick to the cod. If it looks like you haven't got a good crust, dip it back into the egg and the breadcrumbs once more.

Warm a non-stick, ovenproof pan over a medium–high heat. Heat a good splash of olive oil and fry the cod, crust-side down, for a couple of minutes, or until it has just started to brown. Turn the cod over and put the pan in the oven. Cook for a further 10–15 minutes, until the fish is cooked through. If the crust looks like it's getting too brown, just cover it loosely with some foil.

Serve the cod with the warm bean stew and a wedge of lemon.

Red quinoa is better at holding its shape and has a slightly crunchier texture than white, and it pairs nicely with light white fish like sea bass.

190 g/1 cup red quinoa

460 ml/scant 2 cups water

¼ teaspoon salt

1 teaspoon butter

2 tablespoons olive oil

1 large fennel bulb, chopped, with fronds reserved to garnish

2 courgettes/zucchini, peeled in strips and chopped

leaves from 2 sprigs of fresh oregano

2 garlic cloves

2 x 140-g/5-oz. skinless sea bass fillets

2 tablespoons vegetable stock

SERVES 2

Sea bass with red quinoa, fennel and courgette salad

Put the red quinoa and water in a medium saucepan or pot and bring to the boil over a high heat. Reduce the heat, cover, and simmer for 20 minutes. Remove from the heat, uncover, fluff with a fork, then stir in the salt and butter, and set aside.

While the quinoa is cooking, heat the olive oil in a large frying pan/skillet over a medium heat. Add the fennel and courgette/zucchini and fry for 5 minutes. Turn the heat down to medium, then add

the oregano, garlic and salt, and cook for a further 5 minutes. Nestle the sea bass fillets in the pan and add the vegetable stock. Reduce the heat, cover and poach for 5 minutes. Then turn off the heat and set aside for 3 minutes to ensure the sea bass is fully cooked.

To serve, spoon a mound of quinoa on a plate. Plate the cooked sea bass with the fennel, courgettes/zucchini and juice from the pan on top. Garnish with fennel fronds and enjoy immediately.

Fish tacos with chipotle-lime crema

This version of fish tacos roasts the fish rather than frying it. Serve it with homemade guacamole and some crunchy shredded cabbage for a wonderful combination of tastes and textures.

For the chipotle-lime crema, split the dried chipotle chilli/chile and shake out most of the seeds. Dry-toast it in a frying pan/skillet until it smells nutty. Cover it with just-boiled water and steep for 15 minutes. Purée the chilli/chile and the steeping water until smooth.

Put 2 teaspoons of the chipotle purée in the bottom of a blender. Add the crème fraîche and lime zest and juice. Process until smooth and top with a few coriander/cilantro leaves.

Preheat the oven to 200°C (400°F) Gas 6.

To make the fish tacos, dry the fish fillets well and place them on a baking sheet. Cover them with a flurry of coriander/cilantro leaves, pumpkin seeds, a drizzle of olive oil and the zest of half a lime (use the juice in the guacamole).

700 g/1 lb. 9 oz. skinless white fish fillets (such as sea bass, John Dory, barramundi or mahi-mahi)

2 handfuls of coriander/cilantro leaves and stems, chopped

a handful of pumpkin seeds/pepitas

2 tablespoons olive oil

zest of ½ lime

CHIPOTLE-LIME CREMA

1 dried chipotle chilli/chile plus 2 tablespoons just-boiled water (or substitute chipotle powder, or smoked barbecue sauce with cayenne pepper)

4 tablespoons crème fraîche, sour cream or natural yogurt

grated zest and freshly squeezed juice of ½ lime

a few fresh coriander/cilantro leaves

TO SERVE

warmed corn or wheat soft tortillas or tacos (2–3 per person)

Guacamole (see opposite)

4 large handfuls of shredded white cabbage

jalapeños, to taste

salt

SERVES 4

Bake the fish for 10–12 minutes, until the flesh is opaque, or wrap in foil and grill on the barbecue. Break each cooked fillet into thirds (keeping the pumpkin seeds and coriander/cilantro with each one). Place the fish on a serving platter with the tortillas, guacamole, shredded cabbage, chipotle-lime crema and jalapeños, and assemble your own tacos.

Any remaining chipotle purée can be frozen in an ice cube tray, so there's some on hand next time you make tacos, burritos, enchiladas or pulled pork.

Guacamole

The flavour of homemade guacamole beats store-bought versions hands down!

2 ripe avocados

freshly squeezed juice of ½ lime

1 handful coriander/cilantro leaves, freshly chopped

60 g/2 cups good corn chips, warmed in the oven for 10 minutes

6 soft corn tortillas, wrapped in foil and warmed in the oven

salt

SERVES 4

Halve the avocados and cut out any brown bits. Remove the stones/pits. Use a fork to scrape the avocado flesh from the skin.

Mash the avocado flesh with the lime juice, salt and half the coriander/cilantro. Top with the remaining coriander/cilantro and a sprinkle of salt. Eat with warm corn chips and warm tortillas. For a textural riot, combine the two.

A very simple, light dish that packs a hefty punch. You can make your own harissa paste but it is just as delicious straight from the jar. Wear food-safe vinyl gloves when preparing chillies/chiles if you do make your own; no matter how well you wash your hands, there will always be some lingering spice on your fingers, which causes agony if you rub your eyes.

Butterflied prawns with avocado and harissa dressing

4 large raw tiger prawns/jumbo shrimp, about 100 g/3½ oz. each

1 small avocado, sliced

½ small red onion, sliced

a small bunch of fresh mint

1 head Little Gem/Bibb lettuce

olive oil, to serve

sea salt, to taste

½ lemon, cut into wedges

HARISSA DRESSING

1–2 teaspoons harissa paste

2 tablespoons natural/plain yogurt

SERVES 2

Preheat a heavy-based stove-top grill pan over high heat.

Put the tiger prawns/jumbo shrimp on a chopping/cutting board and cut them

lengthways with a sharp, serrated knife from the tail to just before the head. Open up the tail and season with a little olive oil and salt.

Once the pan is smoking hot, add the prawns/shrimp so that they stand on their opened-up tails. Cook for about 3–5 minutes, until the flesh has turned white, then turn off the heat.

Mix the avocado, red onion, mint and lettuce, and drizzle with a little olive oil and sea salt. Place the prawns/shrimp on top with a wedge of lemon.

Depending on how fiery you like it, mix 2 teaspoons of harissa paste with the yogurt (the yogurt counteracts the heat) and dress the prawns/shrimp and avocado salad. Or you could put a dollop of yogurt and a spoonful of harissa on each plate and let your guest manage their own heat.

Pork burritos with spicy pineapple salsa

The sweet and spicy salsa works perfectly with tender, slow-cooked pork.

zest of 1 small orange
1 tablespoon ground cumin
½ tablespoon sea salt
1 teaspoon ground coriander
½ teaspoon black pepper
½ teaspoon chilli/chili powder
1 kg/2¼ lbs. well-marbled pork shoulder/butt, roughly chopped
1 tablespoon olive oil
120 ml/½ cup pineapple juice
350 ml/12 fl. oz. Corona or other Mexican beer
1 bay leaf
2 tablespoons pumpkin seeds/pepitas

SPICY PINEAPPLE SALSA

½ pineapple
½ red onion, finely diced
juice and grated zest of 1 lime
a small bunch of coriander/cilantro
1 tablespoon jalapeños from a jar, diced
1 fresh jalapeño or other green chilli/chile, finely chopped

TO SERVE

flour tortillas
½ white cabbage, shredded
hot sauce, to taste
1 recipe of Guacamole (see page 115)
60 g/2 oz. mozzarella, cubed
60 g/2 oz. goats' cheese, crumbled

SERVES 4-6

To make the salsa, cut the skin off the pineapple, quarter it and cut into small cubes. Combine it with the red onion and lime zest and juice. Finely chop the coriander/cilantro stems and add to the bowl. Add both types of jalapeño, including the seeds if you want it hot. Stir to combine. Add the coriander/cilantro leaves just before serving.

For the pulled pork, mix together the spices, salt, pepper and orange zest. Dust the pork in the spices. Heat the olive oil in a flameproof casserole over a high heat. Brown the meat in batches.

Return all the meat to the pan and pour the pineapple juice and beer on top. Top up with enough water to just cover the meat. Add the bay leaf. Bring the pork and liquid to a rolling boil, then reduce the heat to a simmer and cook, uncovered, for about 2 hours.

Check the meat at this stage, but continue cooking until there is only 5 mm/¼ inch of liquid left in the pot and the meat easily shreds with 2 forks. About 2½ hours should be long enough. Allow to rest for 10 minutes, then shred the meat with 2 forks and toss it with the remaining juices.

Top the pork with the pumpkin seeds before serving with flour tortillas, pineapple salsa, shredded white cabbage, hot sauce, guacamole, mozzarella and goats' cheese.

Rack of lamb stuffed with feta and mint

Lamb is the staple meat in the Middle East, besides camel! This dish takes influences from Persia and chucks a hint of Mediterranean in the mix, too. The lamb works just beautifully as a main meal with some spiced couscous on the side.

200 g/7 oz. feta cheese

2 tablespoons freshly chopped mint

2 tablespoons freshly chopped flat leaf parsley

grated zest and freshly squeezed juice of 1 lemon

2 lamb racks (7–8 cutlets on each rack), fat trimmed away to expose the bone at each end

3 tablespoons olive oil

sea salt and freshly ground black pepper

toasted pine nuts, to garnish

unwaxed kitchen twine

SERVES 6

Preheat the oven to 200°C (400°F) Gas 6.

Put the feta cheese in a mixing bowl and use a fork to mash it until almost smooth. Add the chopped mint and parsley and lemon zest and juice, and stir until well combined.

Use a knife to cut down the length of each lamb rack, close to the bones, about 3 cm/1¼ inches deep, to create a cavity for the stuffing.

Divide the feta mixture in half and stuff each lamb rack with the mixture. Tie some kitchen twine around every other cutlet to keep the rack together, then

place the racks in a baking pan, side by side, so they remain upright. Drizzle over the olive oil and season well with salt and pepper.

Bake the stuffed lamb in the preheated oven for about 25–30 minutes for medium, or leave it in the oven for 10 minutes longer if you prefer your lamb to be well done.

Garnish with the toasted pine nuts and serve.

Moroccan-spiced shoulder of lamb

This marinade works really well with all cuts of lamb. Shoulder is inexpensive and flavoursome, just be aware that it is quite fatty, so try and trim off as much excess as possible. If you want to play it safe, Barnsley chop or neck fillet are good alternatives.

This is so, so easy. Just mix all the herbs and spices together and loosen the mixture with olive oil. Baste it all over your lamb shoulder and leave it for at least 2 hours, or preferably overnight in the fridge. Remove it from the fridge and let it come to room temperature before you start to cook.

Get a barbecue/outdoor grill seriously hot and place your lamb on the grill to cook. As the fat melts and renders, the flames will flare up and char the meat. If it's beginning to look a bit too black, spray a little water onto the coals to cool them. Cook for approximately 10 minutes on each side.

Remove from the heat and leave to rest, covered with kitchen foil, for a further 10 minutes. Slice it into strips and serve, garnished with mint leaves.

1 butterflied shoulder of lamb, bone removed (approx. 1.6–2 kg/ 3½–4⅓ lbs. including bone)

2 tablespoons ground coriander

2 tablespoons ground cumin

2 tablespoons smoked paprika

1 tablespoon ground cinnamon

1 tablespoon garlic powder

2 tablespoons chopped fresh rosemary

olive oil, for the marinade

sea salt and freshly ground black pepper

fresh mint leaves, to garnish

SERVES 4-6

Ouzo lamb pitas
with cucumber, lemon and mint relish

As well as roasting, you can also throw this deliciously marinated piece of lamb on the barbecue/outdoor grill. Ouzo adds a subtle liquorice flavour to the meat, which is enhanced by the fennel.

a 900-g/2-lb. piece of boneless lamb shoulder

125 ml/½ cup ouzo

60 ml/¼ cup olive oil

2 tablespoons fresh rosemary leaves

4 garlic cloves, roughly chopped

1 teaspoon fennel pollen

sea salt and freshly ground black pepper

Cucumber, Lemon and Mint Relish, to serve

6 pita breads, lightly toasted, to serve

SERVES 6

Preheat the oven to 400°F (200°C) Gas 6.

Place the lamb in a roasting pan and, using a sharp knife, carefully score the skin diagonally.

In a small bowl, whisk together the ouzo, oil, rosemary, garlic and fennel pollen.

Pour the marinade over the lamb, rubbing it all over and into the scored skin. Season with salt and pepper. Roast in the preheated oven for 45 minutes. Remove the lamb from the oven, cover and set aside to rest for 10 minutes.

To serve, slice the lamb into thick pieces. Arrange on a platter along with a bowl of Cucumber, Mint and Lemon relish and toasted pita bread.

Cucumber, lemon and mint relish

Fresh mint grows very well in many gardens, and is lovely in summer recipes. This is a fantastically quick and easy addition to the dinner table and works well with all meats, fish, and poultry.

Mix all the ingredients together in a bowl. Season with salt and pepper and stir, making sure everything is well combined.

Chill before serving and store in sterilized glass jars in the refrigerator for up to 1 week.

1 cucumber, finely diced

1 garlic clove, finely chopped

grated zest and freshly squeezed juice of 1 lemon

25 g/1 cup torn fresh mint leaves

25 g/1 cup roughly torn flat leaf parsley leaves

20 g/¼ cup fresh Greek oregano leaves

60 ml/¼ cup olive oil

sea salt and cracked black pepper

sterilized glass jars with airtight lids (see page 4)

MAKES 475 ML/2 CUPS (16 OZ.)

Baked chicken stuffed with asparagus, goats' cheese and sun-dried tomatoes

Chicken kiev for the landed gentry, this looks quite incredible when you slice it down the middle and reveal the cross-section of vibrant asparagus and sun-dried tomatoes. All the hard work can be done well in advance, leaving you free to sip a glass of chilled white wine with your guests.

4 asparagus stems
2 chicken breasts, skin removed and butterflied (cut in half lengthways but not all the way through; if you're unsure, ask your butcher to help)
4 sun-dried tomatoes
4 slices Parma ham
100 g/3½ oz. goats' cheese
olive oil, for cooking

SAUCE

4 tablespoons pesto sauce
2 tablespoons crème fraîche or sour cream
10 cherry tomatoes on the vine
fresh basil leaves, to decorate
rocket/arugula leaves, to serve

SERVES 2

Preheat the oven to 220°C (425°F) Gas 7.

Bring a pan of salted water to the boil, add the asparagus and cook for 3 minutes. Remove and refresh it under cold running water (or a bowl of iced water if you're a really dedicated pro). Once cooled, leave to dry.

Stuff each butterflied chicken breast with two asparagus stems placed lengthwise, two sun-dried tomatoes and half the goats' cheese, and season with salt and pepper. Close it up and

wrap it in two slices of Parma ham. Secure with a cocktail stick/toothpick if necessary.

Warm an ovenproof pan over high heat. For anyone who's wondering, ovenproof basically means that the handle is made of metal, not plastic.

Add a splash of olive oil to the pan and add the chicken breasts, skin-side down. Fry them until one side has crisped up a little. Flip them over and put the pan in the oven for a 15–20 minutes, or until the juices run clear. Put the cherry tomatoes in a small roasting pan and roast for 10–15 minutes, until the skins start to crack.

While it's cooking, mix together the pesto and crème fraîche, loosening it with a dash of hot water if it's too thick. It should be a thick but pourable sauce.

Once the chicken is cooked, leave it to rest for 5 minutes before slicing horizontally, then arrange on a plate. Spoon the sauce over and serve with the cherry tomatoes, basil leaves and rocket/arugula.

Chicken rotisserie

In Provence, a rotisserie chicken is as common as a warm day. Serve this flavoursome chicken with Parmentier potatoes and a bottle of chilled rosé wine. This recipe will happily serve 6 people, and there is no better summer feast!

1 x 2 kg/4½ lb. whole chicken

a pinch of salt

1 lemon, quartered

a few sprigs of rosemary

50 g/3½ tablespoons butter, melted

1 tablespoon salt

1 tablespoon herbes de Provence

1 teaspoon ground black pepper

a rotisserie oven or lidded barbecue/outdoor grill (optional)

2 wooden skewers (optional)

SERVES 6

Season the inside of the chicken with the salt and stuff with the lemon quarters and rosemary sprigs. Pierce the chicken onto a rotisserie set up on a lidded barbecue/outdoor grill or in a rotisserie oven. Set the heat to high and cook for 10 minutes.

During that time, quickly mix together the butter, 1 tablespoon of salt, the herbes de Provence and pepper. Turn the heat down to medium and baste the chicken with the butter mixture. Close the lid or rotisserie oven and cook for 1–1½ hours, basting occasionally. Remove from the rotisserie and let stand for 10–15 minutes before cutting into pieces and serving.

Alternatively, if you do not have access to a rotisserie, a spatch-cock chicken is just as good! Take the bird and, with the skin side down, cut along both sides of the backbone and remove the bone. Press down firmly and open the chicken up like a book. You should find the diamond-shaped breastbone. With a paring knife, cut along both sides of the breastbone. Run your fingers along either side and just pull it out. Thread two wooden skewers in an X shape through from thigh to wing to keep the bird in shape while cooking.

Preheat the oven to 220°C (425°F) Gas 7. Lay your chicken, skin-side up, on a pan lined with foil and baste it well with the melted butter. Rub in the herbes de Provence and tuck in the lemon wedges around and underneath the bird and add a few sprigs of rosemary torn into a couple of pieces, tucking them between the leg and breast. Cook for 45 minutes, or until the chicken is crisp and tender. Take the chicken out of the oven and allow to cool. Pour any juices remaining in the pan over the Parmentier potatoes (see right).

Parmentier potatoes

In Provence most 'charcuteries' and markets sell big vats of golden Parmentier potatoes, sizzling away under the rotisserie to take home.

1 tablespoon sunflower oil

1 kg/2¼ lb. waxy potatoes, peeled and cut into 2.5-cm/1-inch cubes

a generous knob/pat of butter (melted)

any juices or fat left-over from the cooking the chicken

2 sprigs of fresh rosemary, stalks removed and needles finely chopped

sea salt and ground black pepper

SERVES 6

Preheat the oven to 200°C (400°F) Gas 6.

Heat the oil in a large frying pan/skillet set over a moderate heat. Add the potatoes and cook for about 10 minutes, stirring occasionally to prevent them browning or sticking to the pan. Transfer the fried potatoes to a large roasting pan and mix in the melted butter and any juices left-over from cooking the chicken. Sprinkle with the rosemary and season with salt and pepper. Put the pan in the preheated oven and roast the potatoes for 30–40 minutes, shaking the pan occasionally to prevent sticking. When the potatoes are golden roasted, remove from the heat and serve or allow to cool before packing them in a container, ready to take outdoors.

Spaghetti all'amatriciana

This is a simple, everyday pasta. Make more than you think; you'll undoubtedly have a second portion.

250 g/9 oz. good-quality spaghetti
vegetable oil, for frying
50 g/2 oz. cubed pancetta
1 garlic clove, bashed but left whole
50 ml/scant ¼ cup olive oil
1 white onion, finely chopped
30 g/1¼ oz. grated Parmesan, plus extra to serve
a small bunch of fresh basil, roughly chopped
mascarpone, to serve

TOMATO AND BASIL SAUCE

3 tablespoons olive oil
3 garlic cloves, sliced
¼ fresh red chilli/chile, sliced
2 x 400-g/14-oz. cans good-quality tomatoes, chopped or whole
a handful of fresh basil, chopped
1 teaspoon salt

SERVES 2

First, make the tomato and basil sauce. Put the olive oil, garlic and chilli/chile in a heavy-based pan over a medium heat. Once the garlic has just got the first hint of colour, add the tomatoes, basil and salt. Bring to the boil, then reduce the heat to the lowest simmer. Cook for about 1 hour, stirring frequently, until the sauce has thickened. Blitz with a hand-held blender to make a smooth sauce.

Bring a large pan of water to the boil and add salt. Add the pasta and cook according to the instructions on the packet, subtracting 1 minute.

While the pasta is cooking, heat a large non-stick frying pan/skillet over a medium-high heat with a splash of vegetable oil. Fry the pancetta cubes until crispy, then remove. Discard the cooking oil and carefully give the pan a wipe with a paper towel.

Return the pan to the heat and fry the garlic in the olive oil until browned, then remove with a slotted spoon. Add the onions and fry until translucent and lightly caramelized. Add the tomato sauce, warm through, then remove from the heat. Add the Parmesan, pancetta and basil.

When the pasta is almost cooked but still al dente, tip it into a colander, reserving a mugful of cooking water. Return the pasta to the pan and add the sauce. Return to a low heat and stir, adding a little of the cooking water if it's too thick. Serve with a few basil leaves, a sprinkling of Parmesan and a spoon of mascarpone.

Classic pad Thai

Pad Thai is one of the most loved street foods in the world, and it's ideal for warm summer evenings wherever your home may be. If you prefer your pad Thai mild, remember to go easy on the fish sauce!

225 g/½ lb. banh pho rice noodles or flat white rice noodles

12–16 king prawns/jumbo shrimp, peeled and deveined

1 teaspoon sugar

2 tablespoons fish sauce

2 tablespoons soy sauce

2 tablespoons tamarind paste, soaked in 2–3 tablespoons of warm water for 10 minutes

3 eggs

3 tablespoons vegetable oil

4 garlic cloves, sliced

60 g/½ cup firm tofu, cubed

30 g/½ cup bean sprouts

4 spring onions/scallions, green and white parts, roughly chopped

a handful of chopped coriander/cilantro, to serve

50 g/½ cup peanuts, crushed, to serve

1 lime, quartered, to serve

SERVES 4

You'll need to prepare all of the ingredients before you start cooking, as the stir fry process is quick! Soak the noodles in a pan of warm water for 20–25 minutes prior to cooking, drain and set aside. Peel the king prawns/shrimp and mix in a bowl with the sugar. Mix the fish sauce and soy sauce in a bowl. Strain the tamarind mixture and add it to soy and fish sauce mixture. In a separate bowl, beat the 3 eggs lightly and reserve.

Heat a wok on a medium-high heat. Add 2 tablespoons of vegetable oil and the garlic.

Stir fry for about 1 minute or just until the garlic browns. Add the prawns/jumbo shrimp and stir fry for about 2 minutes.

Add the tofu cubes and sear them for 1–2 minutes. Pour over the beaten egg and allow it to set for 2–3 minutes, then carefully break it up with a wooden spoon.

Remove the egg and king prawn/jumbo shrimp mixture from the wok and reserve.

Clean the wok and then heat it up again over a high heat. Add the remaining tablespoon of vegetable oil, and, when it's hot, add the drained noodles. Allow them to fry for about 1 minute. Add the tamarind and soy sauce mixture and stir. Add the bean sprouts and spring onions/scallions and stir the mixture for another 30 seconds. Add the king prawns/jumbo shrimp and tofu, cook for another couple of minutes and then serve immediately with coriander/cilantro, peanuts, and lime wedges.

40 g/⅓ cup mixed black and white
   sesame seeds
2 x 170-g/6-oz. sushi-grade tuna pieces
2 tablespoons grapeseed oil
sea salt and freshly ground black pepper

ASIAN SLAW

250 g/1 cup jícama, sliced in long strips
½ mango, sliced in long strips
100 g/2 packed cups thinly sliced red cabbage

TAMARI SAUCE

1 tablespoon soy sauce
2 teaspoons sesame oil
¼ teaspoon finely sliced ginger
2 teaspoons flaxseed oil
2 teaspoons clear honey
1 tablespoon freshly squeezed lemon juice
1 tablespoon white sesame seeds
a handful of fresh coriander/cilantro, to garnish

SERVES 4

Sesame-seared tuna with asian slaw

Jícama is a great vegetable on its own and, as here, in coleslaw. Sesame seeds are often used for presentation, but they actually give a nutritional punch of calcium and magnesium as well!

Spread the black and white sesame seeds evenly on a plate. Season each side of tuna with salt and pepper. Then coat each side of the tuna with the seed mixture – don't forget the sides as well.

In a grill pan, heat the grapeseed oil over medium–high heat. Once the oil is hot, sear the tuna for 30 seconds on all 4 sides. Remove from the pan and set aside.

For the Asian slaw, cut the jícama, mango and cabbage into long strips.

Whisk all the ingredients for the tamari sauce together in a bowl. Add the slaw and mix it all together.

To serve, thinly slice the tuna steak. Spoon a generous amount of slaw on each plate and place the sliced tuna on top. Garnish with fresh coriander/cilantro leaves.

Thai green curry
with toasted coconut rice

Thai green curry is one of those dishes that seems to be loved by everyone. The trick of an authentic green curry is to get that typical Thai salty/sour tang by adding a large amount of Thai fish sauce and lime juice at the end.

Heat the oil in a heavy-based pan over medium–high heat and add the shallots. Fry for 2 minutes, then add the lemongrass, ginger, garlic and chopped coriander/cilantro stalks (keep the leaves for later). Fry for a further 2 minutes, then add the curry paste and lime leaves. Stir well to combine.

Once the curry paste is beginning to bubble and spit, add the coconut milk. Bring to the boil, then reduce the heat to a simmer and add the chicken and aubergine/eggplant. Simmer for about 10 minutes, or until the chicken is cooked through.

Remove from the heat and add the palm sugar, lime juice, fish sauce, chopped coriander/cilantro leaves and basil. Check the seasoning and add more fish sauce if you feel it doesn't have enough salt.

For the rice, bring a pan of salted water to the boil, add the rice and cook for 15 minutes, then drain and leave to steam for a further 5 minutes. In the meantime, heat a frying pan/skillet over medium heat and toast the coconut until it turns golden brown. Stir the toasted coconut, grated fresh coconut and spring onions/scallions into the rice and serve.

2 tablespoons vegetable oil

3 shallots, sliced

3 sticks lemongrass, bashed

a thumb-size piece of fresh ginger or galangal, peeled and chopped

2 garlic cloves, sliced

a large bunch of coriander/cilantro, with stalks, chopped

3 tablespoons Thai green curry paste

6 kaffir lime leaves

400 ml/1⅔ cups coconut milk

600 g/1 lb. 5 oz. chicken thigh fillets, cut into large chunks

300 g/11 oz. aubergine/eggplant, cut into 2.5-cm/1-inch cubes

1 teaspoon palm sugar/jaggery

2 tablespoons lime juice

2 tablespoons Thai fish sauce

a small bunch of fresh basil (preferably Thai holy basil), chopped

RICE

300 g/1½ cups basmati rice, rinsed a few times

50 g/⅔ cup desiccated/dried unsweetened shredded coconut

½ fresh coconut, coarsely grated

2 spring onions/scallions, thinly sliced

SERVES 4–6

Desserts and sweet treats

Potted amaretti tiramisù

Not only does this dessert look great served in individual lidded jam or kilner jars, this also allows for easy-peasy transportation for picnics. Make sure you pack the jars in a very well insulated cool bag with plenty of ice packs so they remain cool.

6 large/US extra-large eggs, separated
200 g/1 cup caster/superfine sugar
250 g/1 cup mascarpone cheese
250 ml/1 cup double/heavy cream
300 ml/1¼ cups strong black coffee
200 ml/¾ cup brandy
50–60 bite-sized amaretti biscuits/cookies (amarettino, or 25–30 sponge fingers/ ladyfingers, if you prefer)
shaved chocolate, to decorate
unsweetened cocoa powder, for dusting

6 jam or Kilner jars, with lids

SERVES 6

In a large mixing bowl and using an electric hand whisk, beat the eggs yolks with the sugar until thick and creamy. In a separate bowl, beat the egg whites to stiff peaks and set aside.

Add the mascarpone to the egg yolk mixture a spoonful at a time, whisking well between each addition, until smooth. Whisk the cream to soft peaks, then fold into the mascarpone and yolk mixture with a metal spoon. Finally, fold the egg whites into the mixture.

Combine the coffee with the brandy in a bowl. Dip half the amaretti biscuits/ cookies in the liquid, soaking completely, then use them to line the bottom of the jars. Spoon half of the mascarpone mixture over the amaretti bases, dividing it equally between the 6 jars.

Dip the remaining biscuits/cookies in the coffee and brandy and arrange on top of the mascarpone in all 6 jars to create a layered effect, then spoon over the remaining mascarpone mixture. Pop the lids on the jars and chill for about 2 hours. Sprinkle with shaved chocolate and dust generously with cocoa powder before serving or packing in a very well insulated container to take with you on a picnic.

Amaretto cherries

Cherries are the perfect little fruit to bottle, pickle, jam or make into spoon fruit.

100 g/½ cup caster/superfine sugar

170 g/½ cup clear honey

80 ml/⅓ cup Amaretto or other almond liqueur

900 g/6 cups dark red cherries, rinsed and stones/pits removed

sterilized glass jars with airtight lids (see page 4)

MAKES 1 L/4½ CUPS (36 OZ.)

Combine the sugar, honey, Amaretto and 700 ml/3 cups water in a non-reactive pan and bring to a boil over medium–high heat. Cook for about 8 minutes, until the sugar has dissolved. Reduce the heat and add the cherries. Simmer for 5 minutes, until the cherries plump up and are lightly cooked. Turn off the heat and leave for 5 minutes.

Pour the cherries and syrup into warm, sterilized, glass jars, leaving a 5-mm/¼-inch space at the top. Carefully tap the jars on the counter top to get rid of air pockets.

To seal the jars, wipe the jars clean and screw on the lids. Fill a canning kettle with enough water to cover the height of the jars by 5 cm/2 inches and bring to the boil. Place the jars in the water bath. Cover with a lid and once the water has come back to the boil, let seal for 10 minutes. Remove the jars from the water bath and transfer to a cooling rack. Store unopened in a cool, dark place for up to 12 months.

Jam jar crumbles
with Amaretto cherries

Baking crumbles in jam jars has to be the best-kept secret around. Genius for outdoor entertaining and transporting to picnics, it is also a nostalgic nod to childhood, when everything seemed to be served in glass jars.

30 g/¼ cup plain/all-purpose flour

60 g/½ stick butter

2 tablespoons brown sugar

30 g/¼ cup granola

2 tablespoons ground almonds/almond meal

1 recipe of Amaretto Cherries (see above)

mascarpone or vanilla ice cream, to serve

4 x 250-ml/1-cup glass jars

SERVES 4

Preheat the oven to 190°C (375°F) Gas 5.

To make the crumble, place the flour, butter, and sugar in a food processor and pulse until the mixture resembles breadcrumbs. Stir in the granola and almonds and set aside.

Spoon the Amaretto Cherries equally between the glass jars and push the fruit down. Generously top the jars with the crumble and bake in the oven for 20 minutes, until the topping is golden-brown and crispy.

Remove from the oven and serve with a big bowl of mascarpone or vanilla ice cream.

Trifle cheesecakes

These little cheesecakes, served in cute jars, are a cheesecake twist on the classic English trifle dessert. Delicate slices of jam Swiss roll/jelly roll are drizzled with amaretto, sprinkled with raspberries and topped with cheesecake in place of the traditional whipped cream and custard. These little jars transport well for picnics and make a special treat in packed lunches.

Cut the swiss roll/jelly roll into thin slices, then cut each slice in half. Arrange the slices around the sides of each jar and a slice in the base. Sprinkle over the raspberries and drizzle with the amaretto.

Make up the raspberry jelly/gelatin dessert according to the package instructions and pour it into the jars, dividing it equally between them. Leave to set in the refrigerator.

Once the jelly/gelatin dessert has set, prepare the cheesecake topping. In a large mixing bowl, whisk together the mascarpone and sour cream until smooth. Sift the icing/confectioners' sugar over the mixture, add the vanilla paste, and fold through, testing for sweetness and adding a little more icing/confectioners' sugar if you prefer.

Spoon the cheese mixture into the piping/pastry bag and pipe blobs on top of each trifle. Decorate with sugar sprinkles to serve.

1 small raspberry Swiss roll/jelly roll

200 g/1½ cups fresh raspberries

3 generous tablespoons amaretto or almond liqueur

65 g/2½ oz. raspberry jelly cubes/gelatin dessert powder

250 g/generous 1 cup mascarpone cheese

250 ml/1 cup sour cream

2 tablespoons icing/confectioners' sugar

1 teaspoon vanilla bean paste

sugar sprinkles, to decorate

6 small Kilner jars or jam jars with lids

a piping/pastry bag fitted with a large round nozzle/tip

SERVES 6

Grilled figs with almond mascarpone cream

Figs are delicious grilled, but this dish would work equally well with any type of stone fruit, such as plums, peaches or nectarines.

170 g/6 oz. mascarpone cheese

½ teaspoon pure vanilla extract

1 tablespoon toasted ground almonds, or slivered almonds crushed to a powder with a mortar and pestle

1 tablespoon Marsala wine

1 tablespoon clear honey

1 tablespoon caster/superfine sugar

1 teaspoon ground cardamom

8–10 figs, cut in half

SERVES 4

Put the mascarpone cheese, vanilla, almonds, Marsala and honey in a bowl and beat well. Cover and set aside in the refrigerator until needed.

Mix the sugar and ground cardamom in a separate bowl, then carefully dip the cut surface of the figs in the mixture.

Preheat the barbecue/grill, then cook the figs over medium–hot coals for 1–2 minutes on each side, until charred and softened. Alternatively, use a preheated stovetop grill pan. Transfer the figs to serving bowls and serve with the almond mascarpone cream.

S'mores

Here's one for the kids, and for adults who remember being kids. Sweet cookies are used here instead of graham crackers for an extra-indulgent treat, but any cookies can be used.

16 cookies

8 squares of plain/semi-sweet chocolate

16 marshmallows

8 metal skewers

SERVES 4

Put half the cookies on a large plate and top each one with a square of chocolate.

Preheat the barbecue/outdoor grill. Thread 2 marshmallows onto each skewer and cook over hot coals for about 2 minutes, turning constantly until the marshmallows are melted and blackened. Let cool slightly.

Put the marshmallows on top of the chocolate squares and sandwich together with the remaining cookies. Ease out the skewers and serve once the chocolate melts.

Rosewater pavlova

The dessert that everyone loves. Give a simple pavlova a twist by adding rosewater for a scented, perfumed quality — like a summer garden in bloom. You could also try flavouring creams and even meringues with lavender or orange-blossom water, too. If you can find candied rose petals, sprinkle them over the top to garnish. If you are taking this on a picnic, take the meringue, cream and raspberries in separate containers and assemble just before serving.

4 egg whites

225 g/1¼ cups golden caster/natural superfine sugar

1 teaspoon cornflour/cornstarch

1 teaspoon white wine vinegar

TOPPING

250 ml/1 cup double/heavy cream

1 tablespoon rosewater

1 tablespoon caster/superfine sugar

350 g/2 cups fresh raspberries

icing/confectioners' sugar, for dusting

a baking sheet lined with non-stick baking parchment

SERVES 6

Preheat the oven to 120°C (250°F) Gas ½.

In a large mixing bowl, whisk the egg whites with an electric hand whisk until they just form stiff peaks.

Gradually add the sugar, a couple of tablespoons at a time, whisking well between each addition. When all of the sugar is added, continue whisking for 3–4 minutes, or until the meringue is stiff and glossy and stands up in peaks, then whisk in the cornflour/cornstarch and vinegar.

Spoon the mixture onto the prepared baking sheet and use a palette knife/metal spatula to shape it into a circle about 20 cm/8 inches in diameter.

Bake in the preheated oven for 1½ hours, then turn the oven off, leave the door ajar and leave the meringue inside to cool completely (or leave them overnight).

When cool, remove the meringue from the oven and carefully peel it off the baking parchment. Place the meringue

on a serving dish. Don't worry too much if the meringue breaks a bit — there is plenty of topping to hide the cracks!

Put the cream in a mixing bowl and whisk until just thickening up. Add the rosewater and sugar and carry on whipping for a few more minutes until the cream is thick enough to spread.

Spoon the cream onto the meringue, heap the fresh raspberries on top and dust with icing/confectioners' sugar.

Pickled rose petals

What in life is better than Champagne and roses? These pretty pickled petals make any dish or drink look glamorous and summery, and they add a wonderfully heady floral flavour to dishes.

Place the rose petals in a ceramic bowl.

Put the Champagne vinegar into a non-reactive pan over a low heat and warm through. Take care not to boil the vinegar, as it will damage the delicate petals.

Remove from the heat and add the rose water. Let cool for 5 minutes, then pour over the petals. Cover and leave to pickle overnight.

petals of 8 small edible roses
    (about 60 g/3 cups petals), rinsed
475 ml/2 cups Champagne vinegar or
    white wine vinegar
2 drops of rose water (optional)

MAKES 950 ML/4 CUPS (32 OZ.)

Chilled pear yogurt
with pickled rose petals

This is a bright and lively dish, which is great served in small glasses. Adding the rose petals not only makes it look gorgeous, but also complements the gentle taste of the pears.

3 pears, cored, skin on
950 ml/32 oz. plain, full-fat yogurt
2 tablespoons clear honey
2 cups ice cubes
a pinch of salt

Pickled Rose Petals (see above),
    to garnish

SERVES 6-8

Place all the ingredients apart from the rose petals in a food processor and blend until smooth. Pour into glasses filled with ice and top with the pickled rose petals. Serve immediately.

Farmhouse goats' yogurt with pickled rose petals

Goats' yogurt makes a refreshingly light dip and is perfect as a sweet-savoury snack. The rose petals add a vibrancy to the yogurt and make it look almost too good to eat.

950 ml/32 oz. full-fat goats' yogurt
grated zest of 1 lemon
Pickled Rose Petals (see page 138)
extra virgin olive oil, to drizzle (optional)

SERVES 4-6

Line a sieve/strainer with muslin/cheesecloth or a coffee filter.

Set the sieve/strainer over a bowl deep enough to hold the drained whey. Pour in the yogurt, cover and refrigerate overnight.

When ready to serve, remove the yogurt from the refrigerator and place in a bowl. Stir in the lemon zest, sprinkle with pickled rose petals and drizzle with a little olive oil, if you like.

Everyone has tossed unripe or not very sweet strawberries in balsamic vinegar with a little sugar to make them taste delicious, so try it with different flavoured vinegars, too.

Blackberry vinegar

You may be lucky and have blackberry bushes growing wild nearby, but if not, head to the farmers' market when they are in season. It makes the most gorgeous dark ruby-coloured vinegar that is great for cocktails!

Place the rinsed blackberries in a large sterilized glass jar.

Put the vinegar in a non-reactive pan and bring to a boil over medium heat. Pour over the raspberries, allow to cool, and cover.

Place in a cool, dark place or a refrigerator for 5 days–1 month.

Strain the vinegar through a muslin/cheesecloth or coffee filter and decant into sterilized bottles. Store in the refrigerator for up to 12 months.

260 g/2 cups blackberries, rinsed
700 ml/3 cups white balsamic vinegar

a large sterilized glass jar and sterilized bottles with airtight lids (see page 4)

MAKES 950 ML/4 CUPS (32 OZ.)

Blackberry vinegar strawberries
with lavender shortbreads

450 g/4–4½ cups ripe strawberries, hulled
60 ml/¼ cup Blackberry Vinegar (see above)
1 tablespoon caster/granulated sugar
crème fraîche, to serve

SHORTBREAD PASTRY

225 g/2 sticks butter, room temperature
125 g/⅔ cup caster/superfine sugar
125 g/1 cup plain/all-purpose flour

LAVENDER SUGAR

2 tablespoons edible lavender flowers
3 tablespoons caster/superfine sugar

an electric stand mixer
baking sheet lined with baking parchment

SERVES 4–6

Rinse the strawberries under cold water and cut them in half if they are very large. Place in a bowl and pour over the Blackberry Vinegar. Sprinkle with sugar, gently toss together, and set aside to marinate for 1–2 hours at room temperature.

To make the shortbread, preheat the oven to 190°C (375°F) Gas 5. In an electric stand mixer, cream the butter and caster/superfine sugar together until light and fluffy. Slowly add the plain/all-purpose flour until completely mixed. Turn the dough out onto a lightly floured surface and roll into a sausage shape. Wrap in clingfilm/plastic wrap and place in the freezer for 15 minutes.

To make the lavender sugar, mix the lavender flowers and caster/superfine sugar together in a small bowl.

Remove the dough from the freezer and cut into discs about 5 mm/¼ inch thick. Place on the prepared baking sheet and sprinkle lightly with the lavender sugar. Bake for 6–8 minutes until golden.

Remove from the oven and sprinkle again with a little more lavender sugar. Serve the strawberries with crème fraîche in bowls and a stack of lavender shortbreads on the side.

Strawberry and cream cheesecake

55 g/4 tablespoons butter, softened

55 g/¼ cup caster/granulated sugar

1 UK large/US extra-large egg

55 g/½ cup ground almonds

FILLING

200 g/2 cups strawberries, hulled

225 g/1 cup clotted cream (if unavailable, use crème fraîche)

600 g/2⅔ cups cream cheese

120 ml/½ cup double/heavy cream

100 g/½ cup caster/granulated sugar

4 eggs

TOPPING

250 ml/1 cup double/heavy cream, whipped to stiff peaks

200 g/2 cups strawberries, halved

a 23-cm/9-inch round springform cake pan, greased and lined

SERVES 12

Preheat the oven to 180°C (350°F) Gas 4.

For the base, cream together the butter and sugar in a large mixing bowl until light and creamy. Add the egg and whisk again. Fold in the ground almonds, then spoon the mixture into the prepared cake pan. Bake in the preheated oven for 10–15 minutes until golden brown, then leave the base in the pan to cool.

When you are ready to prepare the filling, preheat the oven to 170°C (325°F) Gas 3. Wrap the outside of the pan in cling film/plastic wrap and place in a roasting pan half full with water, ensuring that the water is not so high as to spill out. Set aside.

For the filling, blitz the strawberries, clotted cream, cream cheese, cream, sugar and eggs in a blender until smooth. Pour the strawberry cream over the sponge base, then transfer the cheesecake, in its waterbath, to the preheated oven and bake for 50–60 minutes until the cheesecake is set but still wobbles slightly in the centre. Remove the cheesecake from the waterbath and slide a knife around the edge of the pan to release the cheesecake and prevent it from cracking. Leave to cool completely in the pan, then chill in the refrigerator for at least 3 hours before serving.

When you are ready to serve, remove the cheesecake from the pan and place on a serving plate. Spread the whipped cream over the top of the cheesecake, then arrange the strawberries over the cream. Serve straight away or chill in the refrigerator until ready to serve.

Some pairings are a match made in heaven – strawberries and cream is one of them. Rather than the traditional biscuit/cookie base, this cheesecake has a delicate almond sponge which pairs perfectly with the strawberries. This is a cheesecake for a special occasion.

French strawberry tart

Oh, the delights of a French pâtisserie! Everywhere one looks there are tarts and pastries that glisten like jewels. Luckily a strawberry tart is one of those recipes that never really changes and is rather like a little black dress: it never goes out of fashion and always gets a wow. This strawberry tart recipe is simple to make and completely delicious with the strawberries and cream flavour.

375 g/12 oz. ready-made all-butter shortcrust pastry

550 g/18 oz. small strawberries, hulled and halved

3 tablespoons redcurrant jelly

CRÈME PÂTISSIÈRE:

350 ml/1½ cups whole milk

1 vanilla pod/bean, split lengthways

4 UK large/US extra-large egg yolks

100 g/½ cup golden caster/natural cane sugar

25 g/3 tablespoons plain/all-purpose flour

grated zest of 1 lemon

a 23-cm/9-inch loose-based fluted tart pan

SERVES 6–8

On a lightly floured surface, roll out the pastry to about 5 mm/¼ inch thick and use it to line the tart pan, trimming away any excess pastry. Prick the base of the pastry case with a fork, then pop the pan in the fridge to chill for 30 minutes while you make the crème pâtissière.

Preheat the oven to 180°C (350°F) Gas 4.

Put the milk and vanilla pod/bean in a saucepan set over a medium–high heat. When the milk comes to the boil, turn off the heat and leave to cool a little.

In a large bowl, whisk the egg yolks and sugar for around 10 minutes until light and fluffy, then beat in the flour and lemon zest.

Pour the warm milk slowly through a sieve/strainer into the egg mixture a little at a time, whisking between each addition. Pour the mixture back into the saucepan and bring to the boil again over a low heat stirring all the while until it thickens. Take off the heat and allow the crème pâtissière to cool.

Now back to the pastry, which has been cooling in the fridge. Line the pastry case with baking parchment and fill with baking beans. Put the pan on a baking sheet and blind-bake for 15 minutes in the preheated oven.

Remove the beans and parchment and cook for a further 10 minutes until golden. If you notice the edges starting to brown too much, cover them with kitchen foil.

Leave for 5 minutes to cool, then pop the pastry case out of the pan sides (leave the base on the bottom of the tart) and transfer to a wire rack to cool completely.

When the pastry is cool, spoon the crème pâtissière into the tart case and spread evenly. Arrange the strawberry halves over the tart, starting in the middle and layering concentric rings all the way to the edge until all the crème pâtissière is covered.

Finally, warm the redcurrant jelly with 2 tablespoons water until melted, and brush over the strawberries with a pastry brush and leave to set for 2 minutes.

Serve or, if you are taking it outside, pop the tart back into the pan (this makes it easier to carry) and pack carefully into your cool box, or slice into portions and pack singly in sturdy boxes.

Raspberry and chocolate ganache tart

This tart consists of creamy chocolate wrapped in a light pastry, with a hint of raspberry to fling the flavours into another dimension. This can be made the day before an event and kept in the refrigerator but make sure you serve it at room temperature to allow the chocolate to relax ever so slightly and melt in your mouth.

SHORTCRUST PASTRY

250 g/2 cups plain/all-purpose flour, plus extra for dusting

100 g/⅔ cup icing/confectioners' sugar

a pinch of sea salt

200 g/1¾ sticks unsalted butter, cubed, at room temperature

2 egg yolks

FILLING

250 ml/1 cup whipping cream

200 g/7 oz. plain/semisweet chocolate (70% cocoa solids), broken into pieces

1 teaspoon pure vanilla extract

1 tablespoon chocolate liqueur

25 g/2 tablespoons butter, cubed

200 g/1½ cups fresh raspberries

a 23-cm/9-inch loose-based tart pan

SERVES 8

To make the pastry, put the flour, sugar and a pinch of salt in a large mixing bowl, stir together, then add the softened cubes of butter. Using your fingers, lightly rub the ingredients together until the mixture resembles breadcrumbs. Now add the egg yolks into the centre of the mix and, using a spatula, work the mixture from the edge of the bowl into the middle until it forms a lovely dough. If the mixture seems too dry, you may need to add a tiny amount of water, ½ tablespoon or so.

On a floured surface, knead the dough lightly until it is all shiny and smooth, then wrap it in clingfilm/plastic wrap and place it in the refrigerator to chill for at least 30 minutes.

Once chilled, roll out the pastry dough on a lightly floured surface to a rough circle about 3 mm/1/8 inch thick and use it to line the prepared tart pan. Cut off the excess pastry around the edge, then chill for a further hour in the fridge (or 20 minutes in the freezer also works).

In the meantime, preheat the oven to 190°C (375°F) Gas 5.

In a saucepan set over a gentle heat, very slowly bring the cream to boiling point then remove from the heat and add the chocolate. Use a large whisk to gently stir until the chocolate is melted, then add the vanilla and chocolate liqueur. Stir in the butter, a little at a time, until melted, then leave the mixture to one side to cool.

Prick the chilled pastry case all over with a fork. Line the case with baking parchment and baking beans and pop in the preheated oven to cook blind for 15 minutes. Keep an eye on it and cover the edges with kitchen foil if they start to over-brown. Remove the parchment and beans and cook in the oven for a further 5 minutes. Leave the tart on a wire rack to cool.

Once cool, sprinkle half the raspberries into the pastry case and squish down with your finger before pouring over the thick chocolate ganache to fill the case. Chill for at least 2 hours before serving, giving the ganache a chance to set.

Serve with the remaining raspberries sprinkled over the top.

Exotic fruit salad with fresh coconut

In Asia, sweet things tend to come in the form of fresh fruit, which is no surprise considering all the delectable delights on offer in that part of the world. Serving in a pineapple shell adds a rather retro twist to the classic fruit salad, while sweet coconut milk transports you to a palm-fringed beach with every bite.

1 pineapple, halved

1 papaya, peeled and deseeded

3 sharon fruits/persimmons

10–12 lychees, peeled, halved and deseeded

3 bananas, peeled

freshly squeezed juice of 2 limes

60 ml/¼ cup coconut milk

3 tablespoons brown sugar

100 g/3½ oz. fresh coconut, chopped into chunks

a few leaves of fresh basil, to garnish (optional)

SERVES 6

Scoop the centre from each pineapple half, keeping the shells intact to use as serving bowls. Discard the woody core from the pineapple and chop the flesh into bite-sized pieces. Chop all the other fruits into bite-sized chunks, discarding any seeds or inedible skin and saving any juice that runs out as you go.

Put the chopped fruit into a serving bowl or divide between the two hollowed-out pineapple halves. Squeeze over the juice of 1 of the limes and any reserved fruit juices to stop the fruit from oxidizing.

In a separate bowl, combine the remaining lime juice, coconut milk, and brown sugar, and stir until all the sugar has dissolved.

Pour this over the fruit salad and garnish with chunks of fresh coconut and a few basil leaves, if using, before serving.

Mango syllabub with passion fruit

4 large mangoes, peeled and pitted

6 ginger biscuits/cookies, crumbled

1 x 568 ml pot/2⅓ cups double/
   heavy cream

85 g/⅔ cup icing/confectioners' sugar

seeds from ½ a vanilla pod/bean

freshly squeezed juice and grated zest
   of 2 limes

4 tablespoons brandy

2 passion fruit

SERVES 4-6

Mango is a popular tropical fruit, and everyone will love this dish. A syllabub allows the mango to remain unadulterated so all that heady perfumed taste comes through, complemented by the ginger biscuits/cookies and vanilla cream. This looks fantastic served in glasses or jars so you can see all the lovely layers and colours.

Roughly chop the flesh of 2 of the mangoes, put it in a food processor and blend to a purée. Finely chop the flesh of the remaining 2 mangoes and stir the pieces into the mango purée.

Divide the ginger biscuit/cookie crumbs between 6 glasses or jars, then spoon in the mango purée, dividing it equally between the glasses.

In a separate bowl, whisk the cream with the icing/confectioners' sugar and vanilla seeds, until it holds soft peaks, then add the lime zest and juice, and brandy.

Spoon the cream mixture on top of the mango, then add a sprinkling of passion fruit seeds on top. This can be made 1–2 hours ahead, but keep in the refrigerator until just before serving.

Rosé jelly with vanilla cream

These grown-up jellies/gelatin desserts are truly stunning to look at and absolutely delicious to eat.

Pour the wine into a pan with the rose petals. Bring to the boil. Take it off the heat when the first bubbles rise up. Add the sugar, clamp on a lid and allow to steep for 10 minutes.

Put the gelatine leaves in a bowl with cold water and leave to soften for 5 minutes. Fish the rose petals out of the wine and set aside.

Squeeze the excess water from the gelatine leaves (they will feel flaccid and slimy). Stir them into the hot wine until they have dissolved.

Add the rose water to the hot liquid and gelatine. Pour the mixture into 2 wine glasses and allow to set in the fridge for 6 hours.

Preheat the oven to 50°C (125°F), or the lowest setting. Dry the reserved rose petals gently with a paper towel, then dip in egg white and dust with icing/confectioners' sugar. Transfer to a wire rack and place in the oven for 1 hour, until dry.

Stir the vanilla paste into the whipped cream. Serve the jelly with the cream and the crystallized rose petals over the top.

450 ml/1¾ cups rosé wine

petals from 1 edible white or pink rose

3 tablespoons sugar

3 gelatine leaves

1 tablespoon rosewater

1 egg white, beaten

1 tablespoon icing/confectioners' sugar

½ teaspoon vanilla bean paste

2 tablespoons softly whipped cream

SERVES 2

Rhubarb and ginger

Rhubarb is one of the best flavours in the world, but those tough, sour stalks need some love before bottling them. It only takes a few minutes to cook them in a sugar and ginger water, and they are ready to use.

Trim the ends of the rhubarb and cut the stalks into 2.5-cm/1-inch pieces. In a non-reactive pan over medium–high heat, dissolve the sugar and honey in 475 ml/2 cups water. Add the rhubarb and ginger and bring to the boil. Reduce the heat and cook for a further 5 minutes.

Pour the rhubarb into warm, sterilized glass jars and tap the jars on the counter top to get rid of air pockets. Wipe the jars clean and screw on the lids. Fill a canning kettle with enough water to cover the height of the jars by 5 cm/2 inches and bring to the boil. Place the jars in the water bath. Cover with a lid and, once the water has come back to the boil, seal for 10 minutes. Remove the jars from the water bath and let cool. Store unopened in a cool, dark place for up to 12 months.

675 g/6½ cups chopped fresh rhubarb

150 g/¾ cup caster/granulated sugar

170 g/½ cup honey

2 tablespoons finely chopped crystallized ginger

sterilized glass jars with airtight lids (see page 4)

MAKES 950 ML/4 CUPS (32 OZ.)

Lemon curd tartlets with rhubarb and ginger

Lemon curd is one of the easiest things to make, and can form the base of soufflés, ice creams, and fillers for cakes and tarts. The bright citrus gives vibrancy to this tart and enhances the delicious rhubarb and ginger.

350 g/12 oz. readymade shortcrust pastry

LEMON CURD

5 eggs

150 g/¾ cup caster/superfine sugar

grated zest and juice of 3 large lemons or 125 ml/½ cup lemon juice

175 g/1½ sticks unsalted butter, cubed and room temperature

TO SERVE

Rhubarb and Ginger (see page 148)

edible flowers

10 x 5-cm/3-inch tartlet pans, greased and floured

MAKES 10

Preheat the oven to 180°C (350°F) Gas 4.

Roll the pastry out onto a lightly floured surface into a large circle. Cut it into circles big enough to line the tart pans.

Press the pastry circles into the pans, trim the edges and prick the bases with a fork. Cover with clingfilm/plastic wrap and chill for another 30 minutes.

To make the lemon curd, place the eggs, caster/superfine sugar, lemon zest and juice in a heatproof bowl set over a pan one-third filled with water. Bring to the boil over medium–high heat, then reduce to a simmer. Whisk for about 8 minutes over the heat until the sugar has dissolved and the mixture has thickened. Add the cubes of butter, one at a time, and whisk until smooth, then remove from the heat. Set the lemon curd aside to cool.

Remove the tartlets from the refrigerator, line with baking parchment, and top with baking beans. Bake blind in the preheated oven for 5 minutes, then remove the paper and baking beans.

Return to the oven and bake for a further 8–10 minutes, until golden. Remove from the oven and cool on a wire rack.

To assemble, fill the tartlet shells with lemon curd, then top with a generous teaspoon of Rhubarb and Ginger. Sprinkle with edible flowers and serve.

Madagascan vanilla is perhaps the finest in the world. Harvesting the pods/beans is incredibly labour-intensive, making it a luxury item. This lavish gelato uses four pods/beans but is one of the best ways to appreciate the pure, rich flavour of vanilla. Serve on its own or as an accompaniment to fresh fruit.

500 ml/2 cups whole milk
165 ml/⅔ cup whipping cream
4 Madagascan vanilla pods/beans
160 g/¾ cup plus 1 tablespoon caster/ superfine sugar
1 egg white

SERVES 4

Madagascan vanilla gelato

Put the milk and whipping cream in a small saucepan and heat gently until it reaches boiling point.

Use a sharp knife to split the vanilla pod/bean lengthways and scrape the seeds into the milk mixture. Stir, then pour the mixture into a heat-resistant bowl and refrigerate for 20 minutes.

In a large mixing bowl and using an electric hand whisk, beat together the

sugar and egg white until it forms soft peaks when the beaters are lifted out of the mixture. Add the chilled milk mixture and whisk for a further 20 seconds.

Pour the mixture into the gelato maker and churn-freeze according to the manufacturer's instructions.

The gelato is best served immediately or can be kept in the freezer for up to 3–4 days.

Yogurt gelato

With all the frenzy about fat-free yogurt, we want to propose a recipe based on a traditional whole yogurt — the creamier the better! Yogurt gelato is perfect served with a berry sorbet, or try topping it with honey and toasted almonds or simply with fresh organic fruit.

500 ml/2 cups whole milk

50 ml/¼ cup whipping cream

1 vanilla pod/bean, split lengthways

160 g/¾ cup plus 1 tablespoon caster/superfine sugar

1 egg white

250 g/1 cup plain, full-fat yogurt

raspberries, to serve (optional)

gelato maker

SERVES 4

Put the milk and cream in a small saucepan and heat gently until it boils. Pour the mixture into a heat-resistant bowl, add the vanilla pod/bean and stir.

Place in the refrigerator for 20 minutes.

In a large mixing bowl and using an electric hand whisk, beat together the sugar and egg white until the mixture forms soft peaks when the beaters are lifted up. Gently stir in the yogurt.

Remove the chilled milk mixture from the refrigerator and discard the vanilla pod/bean. Pour into the sugar and egg mixture and whisk for 20 seconds more.

Pour the mixture into a gelato maker and churn-freeze according to the manufacturer's instructions.

The gelato is best served immediately or can be kept in the freezer for up to 3–4 days.

Candied citrus

If there is one thing that should be homemade, it's candied peel. The store-bought variety just sits around and has no flavour or aroma. This may seem a little laborious but it reaps huge rewards and you will never look at candied citrus in the same way again.

6 lemons or 4 oranges or 8 limes
700 g/3½ cups caster/superfine sugar

a baking sheet, sprinkled with caster/superfine sugar

MAKES 475 ML/2 CUPS (16 OZ.)

Peel the oranges into strips making sure you get no pith on the peel. Cut the peels into thin matchsticks and set aside.

Bring a small pan of water to the boil and drop the peel into it. Cook the peel for 10 minutes.

Drain the peel and repeat the process. This will get rid of any bitterness in the citrus peel.

Bring the sugar and 700 ml/3 cups of water to a boil over a medium–high heat. Reduce the heat and simmer for about 5 minutes, stirring occasionally, until the sugar has completely dissolved.

Add the peel and bring to a boil, then reduce the heat to a rapid simmer.

Continue to cook for 20 minutes more, brushing down the sides with a pastry brush as necessary.

Turn off the heat and allow the citrus to cool in the syrup for at least 1 hour.

Preheat the oven to 120°C (250°F) Gas ½.

Remove the peel from the pan with a slotted spoon, shaking any excess syrup back into the pan. Toss the peel in the sugar on the prepared baking sheet, then bake in the preheated oven for 45 minutes. Remove from the oven and allow to cool before serving.

Store in airtight containers for up to 6 months.

Tutti frutti semifreddo with candied citrus

3 eggs
2 egg yolks
100 g/½ cup caster/granulated sugar
500 ml/2 cups double/heavy cream
3 tablespoons Candied Citrus (see above), finely chopped
cookies, to serve

an electric hand whisk

SERVES 6-8

Combine the eggs, yolks and sugar in a heatproof bowl and place over a pot of simmering water. Whisk the mixture with an electric hand whisk on a high speed for about 5 minutes, until it turns into pale yellow ribbons and has thickened. Turn off the heat and place the bowl with the egg mixture over a bowl filled with iced water to cool.

Pour the cream into a large bowl and beat until thick, and soft peaks form. Fold the cooled egg mixture through the cream until thoroughly incorporated. Fold in the candied fruit and pour into a clean bowl. Cover with plastic wrap/clingfilm and freeze until firm.

Scoop and serve with cookies.

The really great thing about making a semifreddo is that you don't need an ice cream maker. It freezes wonderfully in a container and you can serve it either in scoops or turned out onto serving plate and sliced.

Sorrento lemon sorbet

Sorrento is famous for its lemons, which are huge and weigh down the boughs of the trees on the roadside along the beautiful Amalfi coast. Reserve the husks and serve the lemon sorbet inside them in the traditional way.

610 ml/2½ cups spring water

200 ml/¾ cup freshly squeezed lemon juice (about 5 lemons), husks reserved

240 g/generous 1 cup caster/superfine sugar

a gelato maker

SERVES 4

In a saucepan set over medium heat, gently heat 160 ml/⅔ cup of the spring water until it reaches boiling point. Remove from the heat, add 2 tablespoons of the lemon juice and stir in 160 g/ ¾ cup of the sugar until it dissolves. Let the syrup cool for 30 minutes.

Put the remaining lemon juice, water and sugar in a jug/pitcher and whisk together. Add the cooled syrup and whisk briefly again until thoroughly mixed.

Pour the mixture into a gelato maker and churn freeze according to the manufacturer's instructions.

Serve the sorbet spooned into the reserved lemon husks. It is best served immediately but can be kept in the freezer for up to 3–4 days.

French cherry granita

The simplicity of granita is the perfect way to appreciate the season's pick of cherries. With nothing added but pure water and a hint of sweetness, their flavour shines through.

300 ml/1¼ cups spring water
freshly squeezed juice of 1 lemon
100 g/½ cup caster/superfine sugar
400 g/14 oz. cherries, pitted

gelato maker

SERVES 4

In a saucepan set over medium heat, gently heat the spring water until it reaches boiling point. Remove from the heat, add the lemon juice and stir in the sugar until it dissolves. Let the syrup cool for 30 minutes.

Put the cherries in a food processor and blitz to a purée. Add the cooled syrup and blend briefly again until thoroughly mixed.

Pour the mixture into the gelato maker and churn-freeze according to the manufacturer's instructions.

When it is ready, transfer the mixture to a shallow container. Put it in the freezer for 1 hour to firm up. Remove from the freezer and use a fork to scrape the surface of the ice to produce coarse granules.

Spoon the granules into glasses or bowls and serve immediately.

Cheat's blood orange and Amaretto ice cream

This is a fabulous recipe for making a simple yet impressive dessert using store-bought ice cream. If you are preparing this on a hot day, keep your eye on the ice cream as it softens — you don't want to end up with it melted completely!

5 blood oranges

4 tablespoons caster/granulated sugar

250 g/9 oz. amaretti biscuits

50 ml/scant ¼ cup amaretto liqueur

500 ml/1 pint/2 cups good-quality
   vanilla ice cream

SERVES 4

Start by making a blood orange coulis, which will be stirred into the ice cream. Zest the darkest of the blood oranges and juice all of them. You need around 250 ml/1 cup juice. Set aside the zest.

Combine the juice and sugar in a pan and cook over medium heat, stirring, until the sugar has melted. Continue simmering to reduce the liquid until you have a thin syrup. Add the reserved zest then remove the pan from the heat and let cool. It will thicken up impressively as it cools.

Put the amaretti biscuits in a separate bowl and crush them with your hands until they are nicely broken up into approximately 1-cm/½-inch chunks. Don't get over-excited, as they're useless once they become too small. Put the chunks in a colander and give it a gentle shake to get rid of any powdered crumbs.

Set aside about one-third of the amaretti chunks for later. Douse the rest with the amaretto liqueur and stir gently so that it all gets soaked up.

Take the ice cream out of the freezer and tip it into a mixing bowl. What we're aiming to do is let it soften to the point that ingredients can be stirred in, but not to let it go so far that it melts completely. Keep a careful eye on it, since once it's melted fully you can't rescue it by putting it back in the freezer, as it will separate and form layers.

Once you can work the ice cream easily with a wooden spoon, pour in the macerated amaretti chunks and mix until incorporated. Add the blood orange syrup and dry amaretti chunks and stir gently, until they are distributed evenly in the ice cream. Ideally you want the syrup to give the ice cream streaks, rather than turning it all a uniform shade of pink.

Place the ice cream in the freezer to firm up again, then serve.

Drinks

Scottish barley water

Barley water is a nostalgic drink from many childhoods. It is supposed to be good for your complexion — another reason for drinking it, apart from its great taste.

185 g/1 cup pearl barley, rinsed
2 litres/8 cups water
50 g/¼ cup caster/superfine sugar
grated zest and freshly squeezed juice of 2 lemons

MAKES 2 L/9 CUPS (72 OZ.)

Place the barley in a large pan and add the water. Bring to the boil, then reduce the heat and simmer for 1 hour.

Strain the barley water into a large bowl, saving the barley for another use if desired. Stir the sugar into the hot liquid and set aside to cool. Once cooled, add the lemon juice and zest, pour into a large jug/pitcher and store in the refrigerator.

Scottish barley water slushes

Scottish Barley Water (see above) is a refreshing thirst-quencher. Bottle it, and take to the beach, or on a country picnic. Or even turn it into a cocktail with a splash of vodka when the sun goes down.

Fill the chilled glasses with crushed ice. Pour the Scottish Barley Water three-quarters of the way up the glasses, then top with sparkling water.

Drop a lemon wedge and sprig of mint into each glass, and serve.

crushed ice
Scottish Barley Water (see above)
sparkling water

TO SERVE
lemon wedges
mint

SERVES 4

Wild blueberry cordial

Wild blueberries are smaller than the ones that you find in your local store. If you live in an area where they grow, then harvest as many as you can. If you can't find wild blueberries use store-bought ones instead.

455 g/3½ cups wild blueberries
3 tablespoons freshly squeezed lemon juice

SYRUP

275 g/1½ cups superfine/caster sugar
675 ml/1½ cups water

sterilized glass bottles with caps (see page 4)

MAKES 1 L/4½ CUPS (36 OZ.)

Purée the blueberries, lemon juice and 235 ml/1 cup of water in a food processor until smooth.

Bring the sugar and water to a boil in a saucepan over a medium–high heat. Reduce the heat and simmer for 10 minutes, stirring occasionally until the sugar has dissolved. Set aside to cool, then add to the blueberry purée.

Decant into sterilized bottles, seal and label. Store in the refrigerator for up to 12 months.

Wild blueberry summer coolers

This is a lovely way to turn homemade blueberry cordial into a deliciously refreshing summer drink that will be a hit with children and adults alike.

crushed ice
Wild Blueberry Cordial (see above)
sparkling water, to top up
mint, to garnish (optional)

SERVES 4

Fill the chilled glasses with crushed ice. Pour the Wild Blueberry Cordial half of the way up the glasses and top up with sparkling water.

Garnish with mint and serve.

Elderflower cordial

Elderflowers are such a pretty sight — the frilly white blossoms announce that summer is here. These flowers can also be used to make amazing cordials, which taste so wonderfully of summer days.

450 g/2¼ cups white sugar
500 ml/2 cups boiling water
12 elderflower heads, rinsed

MAKES 700 ML/3 CUPS (24 OZ.)

Place the sugar in a large bowl and pour over the boiling water. Stir until the sugar is dissolved. Add the rinsed elderflower and stir to mix. Cover and set aside to cool overnight.

Strain the mixture through a muslin/cheesecloth or coffee filter into a jug/pitcher. Store in an airtight container in the refrigerator for up to 12 months.

Elderberry snowcones

These are grown-up snow cones laced with vodka. Almost too pretty to drink, the ice is crushed so finely it looks like snow. Dress them up with a pretty garnish of elderberries or blossom.

Fill the chilled glasses with crushed ice, then pour a 60 ml/¼ cup of vodka into each glass. Top with Elderberry Cordial.

Garnish each glass with elderberries or elderflowers and serve.

finely crushed ice
250 ml/1 cup vodka
Elderflower Cordial (see above), to top up
elderberries or elderflowers, to garnish (optional)

4 glasses, chilled

SERVES 4

English summer punch

Apples and cherries are a great flavour pairing and have been combined in desserts with great results over the years. The good news is, they work as well in a punch as they do in a cobbler or a crumble.

1.5 litres/6 cups cloudy apple juice

125 ml/½ cup freshly squeezed lime juice (about 4 limes)

200 ml/¾ cup sparkling mineral water, to top up

10 fresh cherries, to garnish

CHERRY-INFUSED SYRUP

125 g/1 cup cherries, pitted

400 g/2 cups sugar

SERVES 10

To make the cherry syrup, put the cherries in a blender and blitz for 1 minute. Put the blended cherries, sugar and 250 ml/1 cup water in a saucepan set over low heat. Heat gently, stirring frequently, until the sugar is dissolved. Remove from the heat and leave to cool.

Add the cherry syrup, apple juice, lime juice and mineral water to a large punch bowl filled with ice and stir gently to mix.

Serve in tall, ice-filled glasses garnished with fresh cherries.

Peach iced tea

There is something rather nostalgic about peach iced tea. It conjures up images of 1950s America; I wonder if Doris Day drank peach iced tea every day? This recipe adds a little bite of ginger and mint to complement the peachy tea flavours.

1 tablespoon China or Darjeeling leaf tea

1 lemon, sliced

a 5-cm/2-inch piece of ginger, peeled and smashed

1 litre/quart boiling water

4–6 handfuls of ice cubes

6 peaches, peeled, stoned/pitted and diced

65 g/⅓ cup caster/superfine sugar

a few sprigs of mint, to garnish

SERVES 4–6

Put the tea leaves, lemon and ginger in a heatproof bowl and add the boiling water. Let the tea steep for 7–8 minutes.

Put 2 handfuls of ice into another bowl, strain over the tea and allow to cool.

In a blender, pulse the remaining ice, the peaches and the sugar until smooth, then pour in the cooled tea. Serve immediately, or, if taking on a picnic, transfer the peach iced tea to a thermos flask. Serve garnished with a few sprigs of mint.

Strawberry slush

Forget those additive-packed slushies whirling around in vats like toxic waste, this is a delicious cooling summer drink that kids will love and that hasn't a sniff of an e-preservative in sight.

400 g/3 cups fresh strawberries, hulled
freshly squeezed juice of ½ lemon
1 teaspoon caster/superfine sugar
a few sprigs of fresh mint, plus extra sprigs to garnish
a handful of ice cubes, plus extra to serve
about 500 ml/2 cups softly sparkling water

SERVES 4–6

Put the strawberries in a blender with the lemon juice, sugar, mint and a handful of ice cubes. Pour in the sparkling water to just cover the ice and fruit and whizz in the blender for a minute or two.

Fill a jug/pitcher or a thermos with ice, then sieve/strain the blended cooler into the jug/pitcher to remove the strawberry seeds. Serve garnished with sprigs of fresh mint.

Strawberry and mint lemonade

Lemonade is so easy to make at home. Here it is combined with fresh blended strawberries and decorated with a mint sprig.

20 ripe strawberries
160 ml/⅔ cup freshly squeezed lemon juice (about 4 lemons)
grated zest of 4 lemons
6 tablespoons caster/superfine sugar
a large handful of fresh mint leaves
soda water, to top up
mint sprigs, to garnish

SERVES 2

Put the strawberries in a blender and blitz to a purée.

Add the lemon juice and zest, sugar and mint to a large jug/pitcher and stir until the sugar has dissolved. Fill the jug/pitcher with ice, add the blended strawberries, and top up with soda water. Serve in ice-filled glasses, garnished with a mint sprig.

Watermelon cooler

A cocktail that is sure to cool you down on hot afternoons. If you prefer your cocktails to be sweeter, you could substitute the vodka for a white rum. Serve with some chunks of watermelon on the side for a complete refresher.

1 large watermelon, peeled and cut into pieces (reserve 6 triangle slices, skin on, to garnish)
125 ml/½ cup vodka
60 ml/¼ cup triple sec
freshly squeezed juice of 3 limes
ice cubes, to serve

SERVES 6

In a blender, whizz up the watermelon pieces, then pass the purée through a very fine sieve/strainer set over a jug/pitcher. (Discard any bits or seeds left in the sieve/strainer.) Stir in the vodka, triple sec and lime juice.

Put crushed ice into tall glasses before pouring the cooler over. Garnish each drink with a reserved watermelon slice, to serve.

Mint tea cocktail

In Morocco, mint tea is synonymous with hospitality; usually this is handfuls of fresh mint and plenty of sugar, covered with boiling water. This cocktail chills the mint tea, throws in a touch of gin and has much less sugar.

4 peppermint tea bags
a handful of fresh mint leaves, plus extra to garnish
2 tablespoons caster/granulated sugar
200 ml/¾ cup gin (optional)
4 handfuls of ice cubes
½ lime, whole sliced
½ lemon, whole sliced

SERVES 6

In a large saucepan, bring 1 litre/quart of water to the boil. Once bubbling, remove from the heat and add the peppermint tea bags and a good handful of mint leaves to the pan. Allow to steep for approximately 3–5 minutes before fishing out the tea bags and mint. Add the sugar and stir to dissolve, allow to cool before decanting into a jug/pitcher and putting in the refrigerator to chill.

To serve, pour the chilled cocktail into glasses and garnish with lemon and lime slices and mint leaves.

Lime and mint spritzer with cucumber ribbons

No one likes to get too sozzled when in the mood for romance, so this mixology is without booze. If you do need a bit of Dutch courage, a measure of white rum takes this from mocktail to mojito beautifully.

a small bunch of fresh mint leaves, roughly chopped
4 limes, cut into wedges
2 tablespoons sugar, or to taste
500 ml/2 cups soda water
1 cucumber

SERVES 2

Put the mint leaves in a large jug/pitcher, then squeeze in the lime wedges, dropping in the squeezed husks, too. Add the sugar and, using a wooden spoon or muddler, bash it all together. Pour over the soda water and mix well to combine. Taste and add a little more sugar if it needs it.

Run a vegetable peeler along the length of the cucumber 3 or 4 times to get some lovely ribbons (discard the first ribbon, which will be mainly skin). Wrap the ribbons around the inside of two tall glasses before pouring the lime and mint spritzer over the top.

Old-fashioned ginger beer

The key to making ginger beer successfully (and to avoid exploding bottles!) is to screw the lids on loosely and keep checking throughout the 3-day fermentation that the ginger beer is not too fizzy. If it is, simply loosen the caps to release some of the bubbles.

2 x 11.5-cm/4½-inch piece of fresh ginger, peeled and finely chopped
175 g/1¼ cups caster/superfine sugar
grated zest and juice of 1 lemon
1 teaspoon active dry yeast

sterilized glass bottles with airtight caps or flip lids (see page 4)

MAKES 2 L/9 CUPS (72 OZ.)

Bring 1.1 litres/5 cups of water, the ginger and sugar to a boil in a saucepan over a medium–high heat. Reduce the heat and simmer for 10 minutes, stirring occasionally until the sugar has dissolved. Remove from the heat and cool until the liquid is just warm.

Add the lemon zest, juice, and the yeast. Stir, and cover with a lid. Set aside in a warm place for at least 24 hours.

Strain the ginger beer through a muslin/cheesecloth or coffee filter into sterilized bottles or into a jug/pitcher. Loosely screw the caps on and set aside in a cool, dark place for 3 days before serving. Store in the refrigerator for up to 4 days.

Tom Collins

Although many consider the Tom Collins to be an English drink, this early punch was actually first documented by Professor Jerry Thomas, the father of American cocktails, in the 2nd edition of The Bartender's Guide in 1876, and has remained a cocktail-party classic ever since.

Add all the ingredients except the soda water to a jug/pitcher or punch bowl filled with ice and stir gently to mix. Top up with soda water and stir again.

Serve in tall ice-filled glasses, garnished with seasonal fresh fruit.

Sugar Syrup To make a basic sugar syrup, put 400 g/2 cups caster/superfine sugar and 250 ml/1 cup water in a saucepan set over low heat. Heat gently, stirring frequently, until the sugar has dissolved. Remove from the heat and leave to cool.

Dark and stormy

This is hailed as the national drink of Bermuda and it is very refreshing served over ice. Homemade ginger beer gives this drink a zesty flavour.

crushed ice
250 ml/1 cup Goslings Black Seal rum or similar
Old-fashioned Ginger Beer (see left), to top up
lime wedges, to serve

4 glasses, chilled

SERVES 4

Fill the chilled glasses with crushed ice. Pour a 60 ml/¼ cup of rum into each glass and top with Ginger Beer. Finish each glass with a squeeze of lime and serve.

500 ml/2 cups London dry gin
250 ml/1 cup fresh lemon juice (about 6 lemons)
125 ml/½ cup fresh fruit purée (pomegranate, raspberry and blueberry purées are all good)
125 ml/½ cup sugar syrup (see left)
1 litre/4 cups soda water, to top up
seasonal fresh fruit, to garnish

SERVES 10

Singapore sling

Created in the Long Bar at the Raffles hotel in Singapore, when this drink is made correctly, and without using one of the cheap pre-mixes that are so prevalent today, it is the peak of sophistication! This is a take on the classic.

500 ml/2 cups gin
200 ml/¾ cup cherry brandy
100 ml/⅓ cup Benedictine
200 ml/¾ cup freshly squeezed lemon juice (about 5 lemons)
1 teaspoon Angostura bitters
soda water, to top up
lemon zest curls and cocktail cherries, to garnish

SERVES 10

Put all the ingredients in a jug/pitcher or punch bowl filled with ice and stir gently to mix. Top up with soda water.

Serve in tall, ice-filled glasses, garnished with a lemon zest curl and a cocktail cherry.

Kentucky cooler

We all know that Bourbon works beautifully with mint in the Julep. This is a longer, more refreshing version, lengthened with grapefruit, soda, and a dash of bitters. Just add ice, a veranda and some sunshine, and enjoy!

To make the mint sugar syrup, put the sugar, mint, and 125 ml/½ cup water in a saucepan set over low heat. Heat gently, stirring frequently, until the sugar has dissolved. Remove from the heat and leave to cool, then strain out the mint.

Add the mint syrup to a jug/pitcher or punch bowl with the whisky, grapefruit juice and Angostura bitters and stir gently to mix. Add a block of ice and top up with the soda water just before serving. Serve in tall, ice-filled glasses, garnished with a mint sprig.

600 ml/2⅓ cups Bourbon whisky
1 litre/4 cups fresh pink grapefruit juice (about 10 grapefruits)
1 teaspoon Angostura bitters
250 ml/1 cup soda water
10 fresh mint sprigs, to garnish

MINT-INFUSED SYRUP

200 g/1 cup caster/superfine sugar
5 fresh mint sprigs

SERVES 10

Mai tai

The Mai Tai is the flagship cocktail of the Tiki movement — a Polynesian theme that began in the 1930s and is going strong today. You will see this drink made a hundred different ways in bars around the world, but this is a classic recipe.

500 ml/2 cups dark Jamaican rum
300 ml/1¼ cups freshly squeezed lime juice (about 10 limes)
150 ml/⅔ cup orange curaçao
150 ml/⅔ cup orgeat syrup
50 ml/scant ¼ cup sugar syrup (see page 168)
pineapple slices and fresh mint sprigs, to garnish

SERVES 10

Pour all the ingredients into a large punch bowl filled with ice and stir gently to mix.

Serve in ice-filled Tiki mugs (if you have them) or glasses garnished with pineapple slices and mint sprigs.

Mojito

The Mojito is arguably the world's most popular drink of the last 10 years and is sure to be happily received by guests. Ernest Hemingway claimed that he drank his at La Bodeguita del Medio in Havana, a bar still standing today.

500 ml/2 cups light Puerto Rican-style rum
200 ml/¾ cup fresh lime juice (about 6 limes)
100 ml/⅓ cup sugar syrup (see page 168)
40 large fresh mint leaves, plus mint sprigs, to garnish
soda water, to top up (optional)

SERVES 10

Put the rum, lime juice, sugar syrup and mint leaves in a jug/pitcher filled with ice and stir gently to mix. Top up with soda water, if desired.

Serve in glasses filled with crushed ice and garnish each with a mint sprig.

Although this drink is similar to a Bloody Mary, the Clamato juice (tomato juice flavoured with clams) gives it a completely, and much better, taste. Seafood restaurants in Canada often add a shrimp as an additional garnish, along with pickled French beans instead of celery. Mott's Clamato juice is quite easy to find in good grocers and online.

Bloody Caesar

30 ml/1 oz. vodka, Grey Goose preferably
150 ml/⅔ cup Mott's Clamato juice
4 dashes Worcestershire sauce
3 dashes Tabasco
1 lime, cut into 4 wedges
1 teaspoon celery salt
celery stalk, to garnish (optional)

SERVES 1

Pour the vodka and Clamato juice into a jug/pitcher filled with ice cubes. Add 4 or so dashes of Worcestershire sauce and 3 of Tabasco and a good squeeze of lime. Add a celery stalk and a lime wedge to serve.

Margarita

610 ml/2½ cups spring water

200 ml/¾ cup freshly squeezed lime juice (about 7 limes), 1 husk reserved

240 g/1 cup plus 3 tablespoons caster/superfine sugar

½ teaspoons sea salt, plus extra to frost the glass rim

300 ml/1¼ cups tequila

pared lime peel, to decorate

SERVES 4

In a saucepan set over medium heat, gently heat 160 ml/⅔ cup of the water until it reaches boiling point. Remove from the heat, add 2 tablespoons of the lime juice and stir in 150 g/¾ cup of the sugar until it dissolves. Let the syrup cool for 30 minutes.

Put the remaining lime juice, water and sugar in a jug/pitcher and whisk together. Add the cooled syrup and whisk briefly again until thoroughly mixed.

Pour the mixture into the gelato maker and churn freeze according to the manufacturer's instructions.

While the sorbet is churning, prepare the glasses. Tip some sea salt onto a plate. Take the spent lime husk and run it around the top of a glass. Invert the glass and press it into the plate of salt to coat the rim.

When the sorbet has finished churning, pour the tequila and salt into the gelato maker and run the machine for a further 10 seconds to mix.

Spoon the margarita into the prepared glasses, decorate with pared lime peel and serve immediately.

Margaritas should always be served ice cold, so using a sorbet base is the perfect way to ensure this. For an authentic finish you could even frost the rim of the glass with salt before serving.

Index

Recipe credits

VALERIE AIKMAN-SMITH
Amaretto Cherries
Blackberry Vinegar
Blackberry Vinegar Strawberries with
    Lavender Shortbreads
Candied Citrus
Chicken Tikka Bites
Chilled Pear Yogurt
Corn and Poblano Relish
Cucumber, Lemon and Mint Relish
Dark and Stormy
Elderberry Snowcones
Elderflower Cordial
Farmhouse Goat Yogurt with Pickled
    Rose Petals
Fried Green Tomato Spice Mix
Fried Green Tomatoes with Summer
    Pickles
Garlic and Mango Madras Relish
Indian Spice Rub
Indian Spiced Lamb Leg Steaks with
    Tandoori Breads and Raita
Jam Jar Crumbles with Amaretto
    Cherries
Lemon Curd Tartlets with Rhubarb and
    Ginger
Lobster and Tarragon Potato Salad
New England Home Clambake
Old-fashioned ginger beer
Ouzo Lamb Pittas
Pickled Rose Petals
Pissaladiere
Provencal Honey Relish
'Put ups' Summer Pickle Brine
Rhubarb and Ginger
Scottish Barley Water
Scottish Barley Water Slushes
Southern Shrimp Hush Puppies
Tutti Frutti Semifreddo with Candied
    Citrus
Wholegrain Mustard
Wild Blueberry Cordial
Wild Blueberry Summer Coolers

MIRANDA BALLARD
Beef and Black Bean Sliders
Classic Beef Burger
Lamb and Mint Sliders
Lime Mayo

GHILLIE BASAN
Char-grilled Tamarind Prawns
Cumin-flavoured Lamb Kebabs with
    Hot Hummus
Curried Pork Satay with Pineapple
    Sauce
Fiery Beef Satay in Peanut Sauce
Lamb Shish Kebab with Yogurt and
    Flatbread
Monkfish Kebabs with Charmoula
Swordfish Kebabs with Orange and
    Sumac

ADRIANO DI PETRILLO
French Cherry Granita
Madagascan Vanilla Gelato
Margarita
Sorrento Lemon Sorbet
Yogurt Gelato

ROSS DOBSON
Garlic-infused Olive Oil and Warm
    Marinated Olives

TORI FINCH
Asparagus and Salmon Frittata
Asparagus Wrapped in Parma Ham with
    a Lemon Mayonnaise
Bloody Caesar
Buckwheat Blinis
Caramelized Pork Ban Mi Baguettes
Chicken Rotisserie
Courgette and Vintage Cheddar Quiche
Exotic Fruit Salad with Fresh Coconut
French Strawberry Tart
Frittata Lorraine
Goat's Cheese, Thyme and Red Onion
    Tartlets
Gravlax with Gin and Beets
Grilled Halloumi Cheese and
    Mediterranean Vegetable Stack
Ham Hock, Bean and Mint Salad with
    a Creamy Mustard Dressing
Hand-risen Pork Pies
Horseradish Cream
Langoustines with Harissa Mayo
Lemon, Garlic and Chilli Potato Salad
Lime and Mint Spritzer with Cucumber
    Ribbons
Mango Syllabub with Passion Fruit
Mezze Platter of Baba Ghanoush and
    Flatbreads
Mint Tea Cocktail
Parmentier Potatoes
Peach Iced Tea
Potted Amaretto Tiramisù
Potted Crab with Melba Toast
Rack of Lamb Stuffed with Feta
    and Mint
Raspberry and Chocolate Ganache Tart
Rosemary Skewered Sausages
Rosewater Pavlova
Salad Jars
Salad Nicoise with Roasted Vine
    Tomatoes/Simple French Vinaigrette
Scallops Cooked in their Shells with
    Thai Juices
Strawberry Slush
Sweet Potato Falafel with Homemade
    Toum
Sweet Chilli Noodle Salad with Crunchy
    Asian Greens/Sweet Chilli Jam
The Lobster BLT
Vietnamese Summer Rolls
Watermelon Cooler
Wild Rocket, Pomegranate and Squash
    Salad with a Balsamic Dressing

TORI HASCHKA
Pork Burritos with Spicy Pineapple Salsa
Fish Tacos with Chipotle Lime Crema
Guacamole
Rose Jelly with Vanilla Cream
Sardines with Campari, Peach and Fennel
Tomato Keftedes with Tzatziki

**ACLAND GEDDES AND
PEDRO DA SILVA**
Beef Carpaccio with Cherry Tomato,
    Basil and Lemon Dressing
Buffalo Mozzarella with Peperonata and
    Rosemary Ciabatta Croutons
Butterflied Prawns with Avocado,
    Harissa and Yogurt
Cheat's Blood Orange and Amaretto Ice
    Cream
Chicken Stuffed With Asparagus, Goat's
    Cheese and Sun-dried Tomatoes
Cod Fillets with Lemon and Thyme Crust
    and Bean and Chorizo Stew

Crunchy Fennel Salad with Pomegranate,
    Mango and Walnuts
Fried Bread Salad
Fruit and Nut Couscous with Fresh Herbs
Gazpacho
Grilled Mackerel, Orange, Fennel and
    Red Onion Salad with Tapenade
Grilled Moroccan-spiced Shoulder of
    Lamb
Grilled Nectarines with Buffalo
    Mozzarella, Coppa Salami and Chilli
Grilled Sardines with Gremolata and
    Toasted Breadcrumbs
Honey-roasted Pear, Crispy Parma Ham
    and Dolcelatte Salad
Pearl Barley, Roast Pumpkin and Green
    Bean Salad
Roasted Butternut Squash, Beetroot and
    Goat's Cheese Salad
Rustic Chicken Liver Paté with Toasted
    Baguette and Cornichons
Spaghetti all'Amatriciana
Thai Green Curry with Toasted Coconut
    Rice

CAROL HILKER
Buffalo Bingo Wings with Homemade
    Ranch Dressing
Classic Pad Thai

HANNAH MILES
Strawberry and Cream Cheesecake
Trifle Cheesecakes

LOUISE PICKFORD
Grilled Artichokes with Chilli-Lime Mayo
Grilled Corn with Chilli-Salt Rub
Grilled Figs with Almond Mascarpone
    Cream
Grilled Fish Bathed in Oregano and
    Lemon
Hot-Smoked Creole Salmon
Mushroom Burgers with Chilli
    Mayonnaise and Onion Jam
Peppered Tuna Steak with Salsa Rossa
S'mores
Squid Piri Piri
Top Dogs
Vegetable antipasto
Whole Salmon Stuffed With Herbs

ANNIE RIGG
Albondigas with Spiced Tomato Sauce
Arancini
Assorted Focaccia Crostini
Chorizo and Olives in Red Wine
Crispy Calamari
Minted Pea Soup
Patatas Bravas
Sticky Spare Ribs with Honey and Soy
    Glaze
Thai-style Beef Salad
Thai-style Mini Fish Cakes

BEN REED
English Summer Punch
Kentucky Cooler
Mai Tai
Mojito
Singapore Sling
Strawberry and Mint Lemonade
Tom Collins

LAURA WASHBURN
Marinated Artichoke, Olive and
    Provolone Grilled Sandwich
Mozzarella Puttanesca Grilled Sandwich

Photography credits

JAN BALDWIN 66r (William Peers & Sophie
Poklewski Koziell, www.williampeers.com), 120r

STEVE BAXTER 4br, 15, 17, 24, 26, 28al, 32, 33,
59a

MARTIN BRIGDALE 117b, 142a, 154br

EARL CARTER 25r, 103r & 105b
(www.tinekhome.com), 160b

PETER CASSIDY 13, 28br, 115ar, 127, 129a, 157b

CHRISTOPHER DRAKE 124

GEORGIA GLYNN-SMITH 1, 3, 5br, 7, 16l, 19,
20, 22, 23, 25l, 27r, 37, 48, 50, 51r, 52, 53, 54a,
56, 60l, 64, 65r, 67, 69l, 70ar, 72, 73, 76–78, 93,
94, 98, 104r, 121l, 125, 130, 131, 136b, 137, 143b,
144–146, 152b, 164l, 166, 167l, 172l

RICHARD JUNG 80, 95a, 96l, 97l, 103r, 104l,
105a, 168

ERIN KUNKEL 10, 14, 18r, 34, 35, 47l, 55, 99a,
101, 110, 115b, 121r, 133, 138, 139r, 140, 141,
149, 152a, 153, 158, 160a, 162, 164r, 165r, 167r,
169

WILLIAM LINGWOOD 159, 163, 165l, 170, 171,
172r

DAVID MUNNS 68a

STEVE PAINTER 57, 60r, 61–63, 68bl, 69r, 85l,
113 l, 134r, 150a, 151l, 154bl, 155, 173

WILLIAM REAVELL 142b

MARK SCOTT 150b & 151cr

DEBI TRELOAR 2 www.lovelanecaravans.com,
4a, 4bl, www.shootspaces.com, 5l,
www.lovelanecaravans.com, 11l, 12, 16r
www.barefoot-glamping.co.uk, 29r & 31a (David
Austin Roses, www.davidaustinroses.com), 41a, 44b
& 46r www.sarah-janedownthelane.com,
65l www.lightlocations.com, 71, 75, 81, 84l
www.sarah-janedownthelane.blogspot.com, 86r
www.vintage-events.com, 88r www.shootspaces.com,
90b, 92bl, 95b, 96r The London home of Sam
Robinson, co-owner of 'The Cross' and 'Cross the
Road', 97r, 99b, 102, 107l www.chambredamis.com,
109, 117l www.shootspaces.com, 122b www.powder-
blue.co.uk, 128, 132 David Austin Roses,
www.davidaustinroses.com, 134l David Austin Roses,
www.davidaustinroses.com, 136a
www.shootspaces.com, 143a, 147, 151br www.sarah-
janedownthelane.com, 154a www.mayfieldlavender.com, 161 The London
home of Sam Robinson, co-owner of 'The Cross'
and 'Cross the Road'

CHRIS TUBBS 68br (A house in Tuscany planned
and decorated by architect Piero Castellini)

IAN WALLACE 82r, 83, 84r, 85r, 88l, 90a, 91,
92br, 107r, 135

KATE WHITAKER 5ar, 6, 9, 11r, 21, 27l, 29l, 36,
38–40, 41b, 42, 43, 44a, 45, 46l, 51l, 54r, 58, 59b,
66l, 70al, 70b, 74, 79l, 82l, 86l, 87, 89, 92a, 108,
112, 115al, 116, 119, 120l, 122a, 123, 126, 129b,
139l, 156, 157a

ISOBEL WIELD 8, 18l, 111, 114, 118, 148

CLARE WINFIELD 30, 31b, 106

POLLY WREFORD 47r, 49, 79r, 113r, 128a